FLIP
THE
SWITCH

FLIP
THE
SWITCH

Activate Your Drive to Achieve a Freakish Level of Success

COACH MICHEAL BURT

NEW YORK   CHICAGO   SAN FRANCISCO   ATHENS   LONDON
MADRID   MEXICO CITY   MILAN   NEW DELHI
SINGAPORE   SYDNEY   TORONTO

1 2 3 4 5 6 7 8 9   LCR   28 27 26 25 24 23

ISBN   978-1-264-26922-8
MHID   1-264-26922-6

e-ISBN   978-1-264-26923-5
e-MHID   1-264-26923-4

McGraw Hill books are available at special quantity discounts to use as premiums and sales promotions or for use in corporate training programs. To contact a representative, please visit the Contact Us pages at www.mhprofessional.com.

McGraw Hill is committed to making our products accessible to all learners. To learn more about the available support and accommodations we offer, please contact us at accessibility@mheducation.com. We also participate in the Access Text Network (www.accesstext.org), and ATN members may submit requests through ATN.

I dedicate this book to my wife, Natalie, my daughter, Michella Grace, and my son, Elias Micheal, for continuing to support the big dreams and ambitions inside me. Without you, none of this is possible. Our desire to help people is greater than our desire for comfort.

To my mother, Melanie, who taught me six invaluable life lessons: We don't whine, we don't complain, and we don't make excuses. We dress up, we show up, and we deliver. These are lessons I carry with me every day.

To all the people over the last 30 years who have called me "Coach," I thank you and appreciate you. Without you, there are no championships to win. You give me my purpose.

CONTENTS

A Message from Coach Burt

The day my life changed forever. It was a Saturday morning in Mt. Juliet, Tennessee, and I was sitting in a workshop taught by a Vietnam veteran whose name was Bob. His role in the war was to wake up every morning in the jungle with no lights and no friends, and just he and a dog would go out deep into that jungle to sniff out bombs, booby traps, and ambushes. Imagine what you would have to tell yourself in that situation. Imagine the mental and physical toughness you would need and the instincts you would have to cultivate. Bob mentioned that the dog had a certain type of drive called a "Prey Drive." This term intrigued me, as I had never heard it before.

"Prey Drive," I thought. "What is that?" I Googled the term and found this meaning: "the instinctive inclination of a carnivore to find, pursue, and capture prey" (Wikipedia). As I thought about this concept, I realized that this definition articulated what I was activating in the people I was coaching and what I had been doing my whole life.

I believe humans to have a Prey Drive, only it's not about killing prey; it's about pursuing a target or goal with a persistence and intensity until completion. From that day forward, my life would be focused on teaching people how to activate this drive so they could discharge the kinetic energy inside them toward some defining ambition.

Over the years, my definition evolved. I now define the Prey Drive in humans as *an instinctual ability to see something either with the eyes or in the mind and have the persistence and intensity to pursue it through to its logical conclusion.*

The Prey Drive is necessary in all parts of your nature: body, mind, heart, and spirit. So to become the person you envision yourself to be, I believe you have to activate both your potential and your Prey Drive physically, mentally, emotionally, and spiritually. To initiate an activity, your physical drive must be activated. To care about something, your emotional drive must be activated. To be interested in something, your mental drive must be activated. To go deeper in your spirituality, your spiritual drive must be activated.

Different people are activated in different ways based on their past scripting and the triggers that initiate something inside them to take an action. The range of triggers is endless and can be found in both negative and positive experiences: A lack of belief from others or an affirmative belief from others. A put-down or a compliment. A slight or a high five. A competition or a game to play and win.

Whatever the trigger, it stimulates your drive to want to do more, become more, and create more. Activation happens when something external turns your "want to" up a notch and switches to a higher gear that helps you expand your mind and your actions. Despite our typical reactions, galvanizing stimuli are a good thing—not a bad thing—which is why you should be thankful for the things that happen in your life (even the negative ones). They don't happen *to* you. They happen *for* you.

There have been five activators that I am most grateful to have happened *for* me:

- **FEAR**—because without it I most likely wouldn't take the levels of action I need to win at the highest levels. Fear is our friend. The faster we figure this out, the better off we are going to be.
- **COMPETITION**—because without something in the future to pursue, I most likely would have stopped pushing so hard after winning championships as a basketball coach; instead I would have been resting on my laurels.
- **ENVIRONMENT**—because those conferences, boot camps, and workshops I have attended and the people with whom I have shared surroundings and experiences have activated and reactivated my drive to reach my deepest human potential. A positive environment is a place where our talents can thrive because of the standards, language, accountability, and atmosphere. Just as we want to place our kids in environments where their talents can come alive, we should be doing the same thing for us as adults. So many environments suppress our talents or are toxic. The right environment could activate our Prey Drive to perform at a higher level due to the expectations, scenery, or structure.
- **EMBARRASSMENT**—because without it the gap between where I am and where I am capable of going would cause me to contract and not expand. Embarrassment could be defined as a painful or emotional state that causes a change in one's behavior. I do not use embarrassment to shame people, but I do

believe as a coach that sometimes in life people should be embarrassed by their lack of commitment, results, or outcomes, and this underperformance in relationship to their capacity should cause a change in their behavior. Sometimes hitting rock bottom or being super-frustrated with where you are activates something deep inside you to come alive. It could take a breakdown to create a breakthrough, or the emotional energy is simply not there to force a change.

- **EXPOSURE**—because being close to and seeing something magical is inspiring. Exposure brings to mind a leadership camp I was fortunate enough to attend at 15 years old—the Broyhill Leadership Academy. The academy exposed me to personal development and a bigger future. Without being exposed to a world filled with accomplished adults who wanted to share wisdom, I most likely wouldn't have the drive to impact others.

Just as I am thankful these five things have influenced me, you too will learn to look to the external stimuli that will *activate* something inside you to do something big in the world. Some stimuli might be the five I just mentioned. Or a dream you can't let go of. The hope is through reading this book, you will be able to look at the circumstances around you, for better or for worse, and learn to use them as tools, as learning moments, as muscle builders and motivators to activate the innate focus, stamina, and talents that will ensure you achieve freakish levels of success.

My kids, my wife, my mother, my father, my mentors and coaches, and those who have always been a positive force have helped me get to a higher place. In their own ways, their encouragement, unconditional love, hard lessons, trust, and honesty have activated my Prey Drive. Throughout this book we certainly talk about the people and the behaviors that will activate or threaten your Prey Drive—the drive that will inspire you to want more from life and to reach your deepest human potential. But we go further and deeper, uncovering many other external factors that will turn on your Prey Drive when you most need it.

Introduction

My journey as a coach actually started by being coached on a local baseball field in the small town of Woodbury, Tennessee, when I was six years old. My coach Micki Vinson affirmed and validated my worth and potential by saying to me, "Son, one of these days you're going to be a great coach." Her belief in me was what I needed at a critical time in my life.

My mother had me when she was 16. She worked two jobs while attending nursing school and raising me on her own. She taught me: "We don't whine. We don't complain, and we don't make excuses." After she'd drop me off at baseball practice, I would stay at that field both fascinated and motivated by Coach Vinson. Coach Vinson activated something deep inside me and prompted me to stay the course and ultimately to pursue my own potential. I would go on to make her prediction of my becoming a coach come true: I grew up to be a coach and have helped thousands of others activate their potential, first as a high school girls' basketball coach and then as a business and performance coach to some of the top people in the world. And it all started with that one external affirmation from that one coach when I was six years old. We never know what will activate a drive in us to pursue something greater, but we should learn to be open and inviting to it.

I accepted a job as a high school women's basketball coach at Riverdale High School, in Murfreesboro, Tennessee, when I was just 19 years old and going to college. Women's basketball was always big in our state, thanks to the accomplishments of the team at the University of Tennessee, led by the famous Pat Summitt, the women's team head coach. Coach Summitt won over 1,000 games as a head coach and 8 national championships, and she inspired many coaches to be their best and to play at the highest levels. I treated my program like it was the same as the University of Tennessee's. At that time my life's path was to win a championship at a school that had never won one and then proceed up the coaching ladder to become a similarly successful coach as Pat Summitt. I was obsessed with this dream, and it was really all I could think about for over a decade.

I began as the coach of the freshman team, and by the age of 22, I had become the youngest head varsity basketball coach in the state of Tennessee at the second-largest high school in the state. With 30 girls a year to inspire and guide toward activating their greatness, I jumped in the deep end of leadership and psychology quickly.

Although we spent hours and hours on skills and drills, it was in the locker room and on the hardwood where I really understood what the game was all about—activating a deep potential inside people that helped them come alive like never before. The game was just the "vehicle" to inner-engineer people to compete at the highest levels and find their voice in life.

I coached at this level until I was 31 years old. Throughout those 12 years, I worked and reworked the motivational strategies, honing the strategies that I use today that help people win at the highest levels in their own life. I tested and retested the concepts and got immediate feedback from the team on what worked and what didn't. We ultimately won 74 percent of the games I coached.

It was there that I learned that to build teams, we had to build the team members individually in their knowledge, their skills, their desire, and their confidence. It was there that I truly learned how to activate people's Prey Drive, an instinct inside them to pursue what they saw with their eyes or in their imagination. It was the ultimate learning laboratory with real-time feedback.

One of the most interesting things that would happen when moms and dads would first drop their 14-year-old daughters off was what they would tell me. They all said a variation of the same thing: "Coach, my daughter has so much potential." They would then outline a list of things their daughter needed to realize that potential, including discipline, structure, accountability, confidence, focus, motivation, and a good coach.

"Define 'potential,'" I'd reply.

They would say, each in their own way, "The ability to do more and become more than what she currently is."

I would respond and give them my definition of "potential," which is "a kinetic energy that is stored until *activated and utilized.*" I would then ask the million-dollar question, "So you're telling me that your daughter has an unlimited potential?"

"Yes," they'd say.

"I have to ask you a tough question, and you're not going to like it, but I have to ask it," I would reply, readying them to look into a mirror. *"Is your daughter watching you reach your potential?"* It always got awfully quiet after that. The look on their faces made it seem like they lost a game of "gotcha."

Nervous laughter and smiles followed, and it wouldn't be until days later, after my seemingly harsh words had a chance to percolate, that I'd hear from the parents again. "You know,

Coach," they'd say, "I can't stop thinking about what you said the other day about what I do to be an example to my daughter."

It's possible you're picking up this book because it's time to get serious about flipping the switch in your life. Maybe you're like the parents of the kids I coached, or maybe you're tired of lying to yourself or others about what you are capable of doing and are ready to take an action toward your true potential. It's time we help you confront your real potential and get real about what you are capable of with your talents and abilities.

Other books out there motivate, but this one activates. I have found there is a significant difference between motivation and activation. "Motivation" means "to move"; "activation" means "to initiate." I believe each day you have to initiate. You have to start. You begin your day with a certain set of actions. You make outbound efforts to grow your business in sales and revenue. You initiate ideas with strategic partners. You initiate follow-up to bring deals to a close. Nothing happens until something is started, and that start begins with you. This is why learning how to initiate is so critical daily to creating a future outcome. You imagine and then you initiate. We can become "motivated" for a short period of time, but I believe motivation is fleeting. I like to call it "cotton candy." It tastes good, but its sugar dissolves quickly. Think of initiation as the ability to kick-start something in your life, to overcome the inertia that has held you back from finding, packaging, and utilizing your talents to the highest degree.

For many, they don't even know what they are truly capable of until their switch is flipped. This was something my wife, Natalie, experienced. From the age of 21 to 24, Natalie was a drug addict, many times using hard-core drugs almost daily, until one day, thankfully, she stopped cold turkey. At 30, Natalie (who was not my wife at the time) found herself selling cell phones for a company similar to Verizon. Natalie lacked direction, clarity, and a vision for her bigger future. Although "good" at her job selling cell phones, this was not her true talent. Her company, seeing the potential in her, paid 50 bucks for her to come to one of my workshops on my book *This Ain't No Practice Life*. She sat in the back corner and scribbled notes feverishly. It was the first self-development workshop she had ever attended. After the workshop ended, Natalie found me and said, "Nobody has ever activated my interest in my own potential like that. I believe I have dreams and goals, but I'm not sure what to do with them or even what they are." I asked her some simple questions:

1. "What do you *love* doing?" This is passion.
2. "What are you *good* at doing?" This is talent.
3. "Where is there a *need* you can fulfill with your talent?" This is monetization.
4. "What is your conscience telling you that you should be doing?"

That one conversation led to Natalie's simple answers:

1. "I love hospitality and design."
2. "I'm great at taking care of people and making them feel comfortable."
3. "I think I would like to start my own catering company."
4. "I think I'm supposed to be doing that instead of what I'm currently doing."

Natalie's Prey Drive—to seek out and pursue—was activated. We would go on to get married and have two beautiful children and an extraordinary life. My wife now handles all the design and redesign of our retreat properties around the country. She handles all the hospitality. She is even writing her own books, and we do couples retreats working with as many as 20 couples at one time on alignment, vision, and talents. That day in that workshop set Natalie on a journey toward her calling—to activating her potential.

THE GOOD NEWS IS . . .

Potential is not specific to an age—it's not relegated to the kids on the basketball court or those "just starting out." I've coached 81-year-olds and 6-year-olds. Potential is in all of us, but it lies dormant. Like a light switch, potential doesn't turn itself on. You need to flip it. Once that electricity runs through the joint, that's when real growth can happen.

My message and my coaching success run contrary to much of the popular theories out there on the subject of success. Many focus on people's skills, believing this is enough. If I just teach them more sales skills, then this will solve their problems. From my view this is fragmented. If we can agree that people have multiple parts to their nature—multiple intelligences—then each of those intelligences must be activated. For example, only teaching basketball skills like dribbling, passing, or rebounding will do nothing if players don't know the strategy to use to apply the skills, nor possess the confidence and drive to implement the strategy to show off their skills. Until you activate the Prey Drive in a person, teaching skills is futile, because the person doesn't have the desire to move toward a target. This is why I start first with the Prey Drive and then move to the person's other intelligences.

The greats learn to constantly look for the things that activate and reactivate their Prey Drive to help them play in a heightened state. What activates them can be anything from studying, watching interviews and videos, or going to events and seminars. Whatever captures their interest. They might even be personally coached by the people who have a skill or talent they become interested in.

The greats are interested in reaching their deepest human potential, which is where you have to start. If you are not interested in finding another gear, self-actualizing your potential, or getting to a new level, then you won't be interested in understanding what activates the gear in you.

Discovering what activates the gear in you takes introspection, awareness, and trial and error. Some people come up with an imaginary slight to activate them—this is where something didn't actually happen but you created it in your mind. You can see this in action in the documentary about Michael Jordan, *The Last Dance*. The documentary shows Jordan, one of the greatest basketball players of all times, constantly looking for anything that would activate his drive. If he perceived a rejection or challenge from others, whether he imagined it or it was real, he immediately went to a higher playing field.

You have to find that which activates your drive to expand. Personally, finding my back is against the wall or feeling rejected, slighted, or overlooked is when I thrive. On the other hand, some imagine a future state and an inspired place. The perfect example is Jim Carey. When he was broke and struggling to make it as an actor, he went to the top of Hollywood Hills and wrote himself a check in the amount of $20 million for his first imaginary film; needless to say, he hadn't been paid $20 million yet. But in time he got to live his dream.

Some people are so motivated to avoid the embarrassment of failure, they compensate with practice to ensure they deliver on the promise. Some people look to replicate what they see the best do; then they try to one-up them to achieve a freakish level of success. Even Jeff Bezos and Elon Musk seem to be in a back-and-forth competition to see who can become the wealthiest person alive—or explore outer space before the other.

I actually practice what psychologists call "mental subtraction." This is where you pretend to lose something you love. The thought activates your drive to work hard enough or take enough action not to have to lose it.

———

Statistics show that almost 70 percent of Americans are disengaged from their work; maybe you are one of them. Stats also show that almost 87 percent of people will live their entire lives and never find their purpose and talent. They show up every day with little to no passion or ambition toward a defining ambition. They are lost and confused and spend days in a state of "randomness in motion." Almost 76 percent of Americans live paycheck to paycheck, indicating they have not figured out how to monetize the talents they possess. Most just make it through the day and through the week with little or no hope of a bigger future. They never even get interested in their potential until something comes along in their lives and awakens them to that latent and undeveloped desire deep within them—like what happened to Natalie. I call this awakening "alerting," and I have made it my job as a coach to alert people to what can be. My hope is that this book will give you hope, that it will alert you to your talents and awaken the spirit of pursuit in you to move toward your aspirations. Consider me a "hope dealer" or an "aspirations enabler."

A CAUTIONARY TALE

I've had breakthroughs and breakdowns that have shaped my convictions on the subject of human potential. The most eye-opening breakthrough came after I gave eulogies at two funerals. I hadn't known either one of them, nor did I know their families. So to inform my speaking about their loved ones, I asked the family members beforehand one important question: "What big dreams did your loved one pursue in his life?"

I was stunned when I heard the same thing in response: "Coach, he didn't pursue any dreams, and he really didn't impact many people. He was just a good person. I guess he lived a good life."

This statement had a significant impact on my life and forced me to get serious about helping others drive their potential and live an extraordinary life. "He was just a good person. . . . He lived a good life" was the general sentiment of both people.

I believe good is the true enemy of great. You don't want to live on planet Earth and only live a "good life." You want to live an *extraordinary* life, one in which at its end reveals how many people you have helped. You want to have lived so robustly, so uniquely, so impactfully, that you'd struggle to pick your top three successes at the end of your life. That will never happen if your drive is not activated to its fullest. Speaking at the funerals initiated my Prey Drive and the instinct both to grow into my potential and to impact others. It impelled me to ask myself some hard questions about regret if I didn't activate and take action.

If the recipe for regret is to just be good, what are the ingredients for a great life? What do you do to activate and take action so you can be great? In preparation for writing this book, I studied some of the top people in the world who have achieved a freakish level of success. What I mean by "freakish" is "beyond ordinary," "fascinating," and "impactful on a grander scale." These people inspire us to expand versus contract, to live lives of impact versus retreat, to truly work the potential they had been given. One such person who has created a framework I think is effective is Amazon's founder, Jeff Bezos.

Bezos had a "good" job making good money at D. E. Shaw & Co., L.P., a global development and technology firm. In the eyes of many, Bezos had "made it," and there was no reason for him to pursue a bigger future. Certainly Bezos was wealthy by working at D. E. Shaw.

But when Bezos came upon a piece of research that indicated the internet was growing at 2,300 percent, he had an instinct that he could use this information to develop a business, and even deeper was the instinct to pursue that instinct. He had a tough decision to make. Would he stay in comfort with a good life, a good living, and a good position, or would he go for it? Would he leave the good life to pursue an extraordinary life? To answer this tough question that many struggle with, he created a formula and framework called the "regret minimization framework," a formula I learned about while watching interviews of Bezos talk about his rise to the top with Amazon. This framework asked one simple, powerful question, "If I were sitting here at 80 years old, would I regret not pursuing this dream?" His answer was yes, so he packed up his car and drove from the East Coast to Seattle to start Amazon, an online retail bookstore where you could get any book you wanted, whether it was in the bookstore or not.

To make Amazon go, he went out and secured investors to start the company. He asked 50 people to invest $20,000 so he could start with a million dollars. Twenty-two invested. As he grew, he continued to take on investor money, giving up more and more of his own equity. With just 16 percent of ownership of Amazon, Bezos would go on to become the wealthiest person in the United States. Amazon would go on to employ over a million people, innovate and create Alexa, change the way you order and receive what you need in the time you need it, and become "the everything store" to millions and millions of Americans. Bezos has even taken people into space with his project Blue Origin.

The Prey Drive is an instinct to see something in the mind or with the eyes and have the persistence and intensity to pursue it. Let's look at how Bezos used the Prey Drive in these key areas:

1. **ACTIVATION.** He saw something with the eyes, the statistic that said the internet was growing rapidly at 2,300 percent. How many other people saw that but didn't associate it with the opportunity to sell books online?

2. **PERSISTENCE.** Bezos raised $1 million from 22 people to start the company. Many passed on the idea, and Amazon didn't show a profit for almost a decade. taking all the money it made and pouring it back into the customer obsession that makes Amazon incredible.

3. **INTENSITY.** Bezos picks a target and attacks it with an innovation, such as Alexa. He scours the world to find

the most talented engineers who can build what he envisions until the product is completed and delivered to the world.

I imagine that right now you have a pretty good life, but is it the life you were destined to live, doing what you love that is both highly enjoyable and highly profitable? Are you helping the people you are supposed to help? Imagine distributing your talent to millions of people and doing well financially by doing great things for others. Imagine closing the gap between the life you hope for and the life you have. Imagine your internal talents coming alive and using those talents to impact people around the world. Imagine your being on the stage, playing in the game, hitting the sales target, achieving some *freakish level of success*.

MIND THE GAP; THEN CLOSE IT

Calling on her unique experiences of caring for people in the last 12 weeks of a person's life in hospice, Bronnie Ware wrote the book *The Five Regrets of the Dying, a Life Transformed by the Dearly Departing*. She found that men and women had similar regrets. The book made me think about what I might find as a top regret based on my experiences with people. I think it would be "I could have. I should have. I was capable, but for some reason I just didn't."

How do people reach the place of such regret? Sometimes it's living for others, sometimes it's spending too much time in an occupation, and sometimes it's just allowing yourself to become complacent. But most of the time, we don't remember our ambitions, or we fail to reach our goals because of the insidiousness of the "current of the urgent." We need to make a living, pay the bills, and navigate through the many challenges life throws at us. Dreams ultimately get swept away by this current, creating regret later in life.

If I could do anything with my life, it would be to help you save yourself from regret, to help you swim out of the nasty current that moves you farther from your potential and from the external things that help you activate it. This book and my life's work are aimed at one thing: activating a drive that is inside you but is *latent and undeveloped*—that needs to come alive.

This book is based on a series of questions that keep me up at night and that I'm determined to find the answers to, including:

- "How do I remove the stress and anxiety in my life and find a path to doing what I love that is both highly enjoyable and highly profitable?"
- "How do I activate and reactivate my drive to find that next gear that is in me but seems elusive?"
- "Why am I stuck at the same place year after year in income or outputs when I seem to be working harder and harder?"
- "How do I find that peace and equanimity versus stress and worry daily?"
- "Why are some people motivated to become legendary and create extraordinary lives, while many struggle to find that motivation and fall into a life of complacency and underperformance?"
- "Why can some break through and many can't?"

I've struggled with these questions most of my life, first as a championship basketball coach and now as a business coach. And in my jobs, I've worked with people around the world in small businesses and big corporations. I've worked with everyone from maximum security prisoners, to CEOs worth hundreds of millions of dollars, to hourly wage workers, to kids and parents. What I have discovered is that at the end of the day, we all have a drive inside us that, if found and activated, can change everything.

My mission is finding the stimulus that activates and alerts my clients and players. I call it "flipping the switch." When this switch is flipped on in people, they become activated and ready to take action at a ridiculously higher level. It is at this level of alertness—when we are motivated, engaged, and, of course, driven—that we all perform at a higher frequency. I help people answer life-changing questions that help bring clarity to their future. In particular, I have them ask themselves these four questions:

1. "How do I find my unique talents in the world that separate me?" I call this your "special."

2. "How do I 'package' my unique talents into distribution channels so that others can experience these talents and use them to solve their problems?"

3. "How do I 'market and promote' my unique talents to people who desperately need them?"

4. "How do I monetize my talents by distributing them to the world through my work and potentially make millions with them, just as an artist, athlete, or entertainer does?"

The unique process of helping people get total clarity on the gap between the life they have and the life they would like to have is critical to closing the gap. This process, explored throughout this book, will go deep into such questions and much more to help you understand and activate your Prey Drive daily—and even notice how to activate it in others as a leader or influencer.

MAJOR ACTIVATORS

When I was a 25-year-old high school basketball coach, I felt stuck. My team was no better. We were not operating at a high level, and we had just lost a game. The players seemed sluggish, unmotivated, and complacent. I had used fear to try to motivate them by using consequence-based coaching. If they didn't perform to their potential or execute, there was always a negative consequence. Sometimes I would impose a punishment like running. Sometimes I would resort to yelling or embarrassing. Sometimes I meted out a team punishment that created peer pressure. These were the only things I knew to do at the time, because that's how my coaches motivated me when I was younger. But it wasn't working.

And then I thought back to my first coach, Micki Vinson. She was tough and disciplined, but I remember her affirming and validating my worth and potential in such clear ways that I began to see those traits in myself. "Could there be another way to motivate them?" I asked myself. I would eventually work on becoming a master at understanding and activating the drive to win, one player at a time—and many more people beyond that in the years to come. If you are building a team, you have to take the time to find what motivates each team player and connect the player to it. That's how championships are won: by building a strong and personal connection with each player one at a time. To flip the switch, you have to understand people's primary drivers and the phases of the Prey Drive that they struggle with.

Not everyone is motivated by fear (and I have since come to believe motivating through fear is a short-term solution to a long-term problem). So the following season, instead of using just fear as a motivator, I used other various drivers to see what would work for each player. (I'll share more about each driver later in the book.) Each discovery activated a new gear, and it didn't take long to have a highly competitive, motivated team that was singularly focused on winning a championship and executing without distraction.

When the championship game came around, I turned it up even higher. We had made it to the championships before, but we had been beaten every time. This year, though, I added a new tactic. I bought faux championship rings for the players to wear as inspiration (*exposure*). I brought in gold basketballs so they could see what we would win (*environment*). I photoshopped pictures of the team standing in the arena in front of 10,000 cheering fans. I exposed the kids to what it would be like if they were to win, which is different from telling them or even scaring them. They could now feel the win viscerally. It was imprinted in their hearts and in their minds. It was deep in their spirit. We were in one accord as I, the coach, had worked harder to understand them. I was now one of them, not separate from them.

That was the year we won the title. It was also the beginning of my journey to build a championship program and to master how to activate the drive in another person. My team had gone from just having drive to activating the Prey Drive, and this is an important distinction. Up until this point much of the drive had gone from me to them. Now the players on the team had figured out how to activate it in themselves. There was ownership of the Prey Drive.

The drive was internal. It was a deeper level of activation and commitment with a laserlike focus and intensity toward a defining ambition. Although other teams had worked hard, they had not achieved this freakish level of success. Looking back, it was so much deeper than just being motivated. The vision of being the best, winning a championship, and achieving something extraordinary seemed to awaken a new desire from within that couldn't be suppressed. It was an amazing thing to watch. Very few will dig this deep or push this hard, but this was our intention, to experience the moment of a decade to be the best.

Tim Grover, my good friend and author of the book *Winning: The Unforgiving Race to Greatness*, writes that winning is about the years of preparation it takes for the 30 seconds of celebration you feel when you win. I wouldn't trade the 30 seconds I had standing in the middle of that court in front of 10,000 fans for anything. It was all worth it. If you are coaching a team, never underestimate the need to activate and reactivate your players' drive daily. This is a far bigger task than teaching them a skill. It is activating the killer instinct inside them to even pursue the target.

IN PURSUIT OF HAPPINESS

At the beginning of this Introduction, I told you a story about Bob, a Vietnam vet, and his dog, and I said that Bob introduced me to the notion of the Prey Drive. In researching the term, I was fascinated to learn that it's not actually capturing the prey that motivates the dog; it's pursuing the prey, an instinct so strong that no external force becomes necessary to motivate the animal. *The reward is in the pursuit.*

The big revelation is that the sense of pursuit is also what motivates humans. Yes, it is satisfying to *accomplish* a goal. But that sense of accomplishment goes away quickly and so no longer satisfies. We long to hunt again for the next big score, the next big play, the next big championship. This is why the pursuit of the potential is more important than the actual realization of it. It expands us in a never-ending cycle of growth.

Because of that, I almost titled this book *The Chase*. The real activation and persistence and enjoyment comes from the pursuit of a big target that gets you excited. This is what I am hoping to help you do: get to a point where you take great pleasure in the pursuit, whether you win or lose. Those who operate at the highest levels of our society wake up in the morning and "pursue" something great. The pursuit is what motivates and excites them just like the dog when it knows it gets to go and hunt.

WHAT TO EXPECT FROM THIS BOOK

To write this book, I deeply studied the top 20 motivational theories. I deconstructed those theories into small chunks that would help me research what activates the drive in people. Most motivational theories say the same thing; *We move toward things we want.* But what happens when we no longer want anything because our basic needs are met? We settle. We retreat. We shy away from anything that would make us uncomfortable. We become complacent. This book is going to teach you how to achieve a maximum level of performance instead of existing in a state of mediocrity or boredom.

The book is structured around the five drivers of the Prey Drive—fear, competition, environment, embarrassment, and exposure—within each of the three phases—activation, persistence, and intensity. Throughout the book you will hear much more about the five drivers, the science behind each, stories and anecdotes from my work, and interviews with freakishly successful people who have achieved the potential in them.

My hope is that this book will serve as your "alert" to your potential and be the road map to activate it. No longer will you be the person who has a lot of talent but not the drive to activate. This book will possibly challenge you in ways that you have not been challenged and open your eyes to a bigger and more successful world. I believe the Prey Drive is in you waiting to be activated and reactivated. I encourage you to allow this book to be your coach and hope you will use the tools provided and my 30 years of experience to dig in and go pro with your potential.

FLIP
THE
SWITCH

CHAPTER 1

Motivated by What?

The Three Phases of the Prey Drive

> *Every person who wins in any undertaking*
> *must be willing to burn his ships and cut all*
> *sources of retreat. Only by so doing can one be*
> *sure of maintaining that state of mind known*
> *as a burning desire to win, essential to success.*
> —NAPOLEON HILL

In March 2020 I was running a successful coaching business. That business was in the top 0.0001 percent of money generators in the world of coaches. I was hitting a stride after devoting over two decades to building something special and profitable. I was having fun doing exactly what I was supposed to be doing on earth. This was my "voice and calling." Then out of nowhere an external event happened—a worldwide pandemic. The pandemic caused the cancellation of many live events where I marketed and sold my coaching. In a typical year I would speak as many as 200 times around the world, putting me in front of thousands of people and generating thousands of leads for my salespeople to work. But suddenly there were no events.

During this period my own team went into a deep depression. How could we be in the motivation business and be totally unmotivated? My team members were used to flying on private jets, being around some of the coolest people in the world, seeing some of the best cities, staying in luxurious hotels, and having a constant external stimulus that made the exhausting 18-hour days they were used to "fun and exciting." My team and I were used to living in an inspired state, but all that inspiration suddenly turned into low negative energy toward each other. And I had become negative and cynical, which was only making matters worse. I was desperately searching for something to happen to change my state of energy and move us in a new direction.

I was helplessly watching years of building a multimillion-dollar business come to a halt. It terrified me. For a minute I pouted. I whined. I complained. I blamed. But for just a minute. I knew from being a coach for 30 years that none of that was the answer. I also remembered these were exactly the behaviors my mother said we "don't do."

Everything I had worked for was in jeopardy—and I'm sure you and many of the people you know experienced the same thing. I was afraid. I was afraid I'd lose all my hard work, my clients, my calling in life.

Then reality smacked me right upside the head. I realized that to get a new result in life, you need a new preparation. You can't get a new result with an old preparation. No longer could my old level of performance get us to the next level. This new reality was exactly what I needed to shift gears and unleash a whole new creativity that would be needed to win in a new economy.

And then I did maybe the most creative thing I'd ever done in my life. I acknowledged all my fear that had spun me into despair and then trickled onto my team, and I made myself use that fear. I told myself how much I loved fear, how the unknown challenged me. I did this over and over again until my brain gave up fighting me on it and began to believe it.

The fear galvanized me, as now I had a game to play, a competition to win, a nemesis to cut down and reshape. Nothing can change until you cut away the things that keep you stuck. For me, I had to make the decision to cut away the fear-based actions (like blaming and sulking) that do nothing to achieve momentum.

Complaining, making excuses, blaming, and sulking are all things we do when we are reacting with fear; they are avoidance mechanisms. Our brains are wired to help us avoid what is dangerous, so consciously fighting these fear-based actions is part of nurturing the Prey Drive. I decided to cut away any fear and reframe it by using fear as a motivator instead of a deterrent.
This is not the typical way people view fear. We hear many more stories about fear paralyzing people, making them do nothing. But how does doing nothing solve your sales problem? How does doing nothing solve your weight problem? How does doing nothing solve your confusion about your talent and potential? It doesn't. Taking an action does.

So this is our motto: *When in doubt, take an action.* An action is to pick up the phone, send a text, call a client, engage with your top influencers, follow up on a lead, create a video. Taking an action and creating some new energy will never lead you wrong because it gets you out of a funk and motivates you into movement.

ACT OR REACT? YOU DECIDE

At the age of 18, I first learned about the work of Dr. Stephen Covey, best known for his book *The 7 Habits of Highly Effective People*. His teachings deeply scripted in me how important it is to activate the potential in the whole person: *body, mind, heart, and spirit. Potential* being kinetic energy that is stored until utilized.

Covey believed that "the essence of being human is to direct your own life. Humans act; animals react. Humans can make decisions based on their values. Your power to choose the direction of your life allows you to reinvent yourself, to change your future, and to powerfully influence the rest of your creation."[1]

Notice the key phrases there:

- "Direct your own life."
- "Make decisions."
- "Reinvent yourself."

Covey also believed, "Between stimulus [what happens to you] and response [how you choose to respond to what happens to you] there is a space. In that space lies our freedom and power to choose our response. In these choices lie our growth and happiness."[2] How was I going to respond in 2020? Well, I knew how I was reacting: complaining, overthinking, not sleeping. Reaction lacks control; response is controlled. My response needed to be clear, tangible, and measurable.

The economy is an external factor. The pandemic is an external factor. The government is an external factor. They are not me, not my business, not my clients, not my life's ambition.

All I could control was my response to what happened to me and preserve the things that my Prey Drive had been targeting day after day, year after year. I could control my actions daily, my attitude, and my "usage" of this adversity. To get out of the mess I was in, I decided that I was going to *multiply* everything I was doing, because taking action versus complaining always served me well in life.

I made a decision I would do as many Zoom coaching calls as I could. I decided that I would offer free coaching to anyone who wanted it to stimulate leads. And I made a decision that I would do a live video every day through social media to keep people moving in a forward direction. I cut away my feelings of fear and let feelings of action cut in. I made fear my best friend instead of my captor. I used fear to motivate me to take tremendous amounts of new action. Many of the things I started doing were things I really should have been doing all along but had grown complacent of. In that way, fear became my radar, leading back to my best, most productive self.

Finding Your Activator

Over the next six months of 2020, my team and I worked harder than ever. Members of my team even made comments like, "We've never seen you at these levels," and "What has happened to you?" I was back on my game, and I now had a fight to win, a trophy to pursue, a championship to claim. I wasn't going to let the pandemic ruin what I had worked so hard to build for years. I was *fighting mad*, and *I was facing my fear*, and this rubbed off on my team. The pent-up anger we were taking out on ourselves and, at times, on each other slowly became our rallying cry. And the overwhelming fear was funneled into action.

Typically, fear is an emotion that tells us that something or someone is going to harm us in the future. The pandemic made me fear that I would lose everything. In that way the fear of loss was a primary activator of my Prey Drive. It was the external factor that triggered the thought of "Hey, I want this to change." Recognizing my activator forced me to transform my business and bring back creativity and resourcefulness. It forced me to work muscles I hadn't worked in years.

Whether imagined or real, fear activates us many times to move. With this understanding, you can learn to view unfortunate moments as the activator of your Prey Drive, igniting a fighting spirit that is deep within you but has gone dim or dormant.

I wish I could tell it's easy to activate your Prey Drive when things are good, but unfortunately that is not the nature of the Prey Drive. It takes passion to push us from dim or dormant into a state of action, and real passion comes from conflict. Internal conflict. External conflict. Philosophical conflict. As examples:

Internal conflict would include fear, insecurity, worry, anxiety, doubt, and lack of self-worth.

External conflict could be the need for money or material things to bring something to your life.

Philosophical conflict might be a sense of right or wrong or a sense of justice. Or it might be deep core values you have internalized based on the way you were raised and possibly the differences in how you see the world and how another sees the world.

A good conflict can actually activate your Prey Drive like you can't imagine. You now have something to prove with a new energy and a new emotion.

Think back to a time in your life when you were on *fire*. When you were operating at a higher level than normal. You were in a flow, had a rhythm, and had a momentum, and it was so obvious, that other people recognized this in you. Something happened inside you to cause a shift in your behavior.

Over my 30 years of coaching, I have seen how, for many, this shift is for a short season. The common tendency of humans is to start with good intentions, fall off the wagon, and then experience guilt. I believe the guilt is associated with grief. We are grieving our lost potential. This vicious cycle stops dreams before they manifest, prohibits mastery, and keeps millions of people around the world stuck in a rut and in a complacent state.

When was the last time you got "fighting mad"? I mean mad enough that you actually *did* something? Followed through, got creative, stayed up at night trying to figure something out? This is the type of drive you need if you want to avoid getting stuck living a comfortable life with a comfortable schedule doing comfortable things. To utilize the conflicts and negative experiences, I encourage you to:

1. **MAKE UP YOUR MIND THAT THINGS DON'T HAPPEN *TO* YOU.** They happen *for* you: they stimulate your growth to a new level. And those would be the good things, the bad things, and all the other things.

2. **LEARN TO USE ADVERSITY TO ACCELERATE PROGRESS.** Very few people are operating at a high level, because there is nothing there to push them. The fear of going back to an old way of living, losing everything you have, downgrading your lifestyle, or being embarrassed can be a powerful stimulant to a bigger future. Adversity is stimulus. It prompts you to think and act versus stagnate. Frustration can be your friend if it prods you to get up and initiate.

7

3. **LEARN TO USE FRUSTRATION AS FUEL TO *TAKE* ACTION VERSUS *TALK ABOUT* ACTION.** You can talk about wanting to get to another level all day long, but for me I must get sick and tired of something before I take action. I need to feel the frustration so deep and be so sick of it that it causes an anger. The anger then turns into fuel for action.

4. **CATCH YOURSELF IN ANY LOW-VALUE ACTIVITY THAT DOES NOT PRODUCE MONEY OR MOMENTUM TOWARD THE TARGET.** Our lives are filled with distractions away from the primary targets. Conversations, social media, dramas, other people's problems, and current events all serve as mental roadblocks. Don't allow the distractions and low-level energy of others derail you, diverting you from your goals and dreams.

5. **MOVE FROM BEING THE VICTIM TO BEING THE VICTOR.** The victim asks, "Why me?" The victor asks, "What is this trying to teach me?" The victim blames; the victor utilizes. The victim pouts; the victor acts. The victim lies down; the victor gets up.

Each of these steps requires you to make a conscious decision to "use" whatever comes your way to your benefit versus your detriment. This is a conscious decision and leads to the activation of the Prey Drive. Without the stimulus, without the pain, without the energy, you simply move to a set point and accept your current realities. Go to a place in your life right now you are disgusted with and sick and tired of. This book will help motivate you to action to turn this area around. But first let's look at what really makes up your Prey Drive.

THE THREE PHASES OF THE PREY DRIVE IN DETAIL

We were born with a drive to pursue; just look at any child who is curious about everything and gets restless when that pursuit of something new is prevented. This is the Prey Drive, *an instinctual ability to see something we want and pursue it with an intensity and a persistence.*

The Prey Drive is not something you turn on and leave on autopilot. It takes work, time, and iteration. It requires three phases and your commitment to work each phase repeatedly and to recognize when to move to the next phase.

The three phases, first mentioned in the Introduction, are *activation*, *persistence*, and *intensity*. Briefly, activation involves identifying your activator and knowing how to activate daily. Persistence means you need to "work the muscle" (a metaphor for doing something daily you don't want to do) to become great over long cycles of time. Intensity is being ferocious, playing offense, and showing up prepared.

Let's dive deeper into each.

Activation

The switch is flipped. In this phase your senses come alive. Your imagination is awakened. You are now interested in your potential, maybe for the first time in your life. This activation can be created by an external factor such as a video you watch that awakens your potential, or a pandemic threatening your business, or a meeting that was on your schedule but you totally forgot. It could be activated through exposure to someone who thinks at a higher level or frequency and enlightens you to a new concept. It could be activated through exercise when your body is producing certain biochemicals that awaken you to something new. The important thing is that you become aware of what can activate your drive and you place yourself in a position to receive this activation.

Persistence

Persistence to me is the ability to work the muscle—to soldier on against your inclination not to do so. It's the ability to subordinate what you want now to get what you want eventually. It's the ability to persist and to keep going even when things become monotonous. In the sales world it's the ability to prospect daily, follow up, and see something through to a closure. Once the drive is activated, it is then important to build the muscle and discipline it takes to see that drive through to its conclusion.

Think of it this way: motivation starts the ball rolling, and discipline finishes it. The motivation part is the activation of the drive. The discipline part is the self-discipline you need to take the motivation and see it through to its conclusion. This means you can take a thought, an idea, or a stimulus you have and work it until it is completed. This would equate to your daily actions to build the mental and physical muscles you need to go all the way to a conclusion.

In the sales world this is making the one extra phone call, staying the extra hour, going until you hit your target without quitting. Very few have this kind of discipline. Yet it is this kind of discipline that separates winners from losers.

I believe that talent, of course, is important, but not as important as grit. Grit wins, and grit is built through the daily small disciplines over long cycles of time, where the work ethic becomes ingrained in who you are. Interestingly, in his book *The Art of the Impossible*, Steven Kotler goes deeper into the physiology of what is actually happening inside the body over a cycle of time. What he found was at a certain point, muscle memory literally becomes part of the structure of the cells.

Intensity

Intensity is ferocity; it is zeal. It is how hard you attack a dream, a target, a goal. Intensity happens first in the mind and imagination. You visualize it, see it. You then transfer that into the physical world with a series of actions that are coordinated with each other toward an ideal outcome. In our coaching programs we call this "going from A to B"—the intensity is locking in on a final target and pushing toward that final target with fervor. It's a push. It's on a timeline. It's urgent and important. Very few in our society enter this phase. They approach goals as if "maybe they will happen." They do not lock in on an ideal outcome and do whatever it takes to achieve that target.

Many can activate their drive if they are in the right environments and exposed to the right things. Phases two and three are the areas most struggle in. Few have the toughness to go all the way and often give in to their amateur desires. In a study of top financial advisors at one major firm, Dr. Kevin Elko, team psychologist for the University of Alabama football team and top business consultant, discovered one key trait of all the top performers: the ability to lock into and keep coming back to the target. If you are lacking this intensity (and most are), this is an area we need to tackle.

In the Introduction, I shared with you how I locked into the goal of winning a championship as a 22-year-old coach. I didn't win one until nine years later but stayed the course. It was a nine-year, 80-hour-per-week journey toward one outcome, winning a championship. I had to sacrifice a lot. I wouldn't allow distraction to pull me away. I came in on Saturday mornings and Sunday afternoons and worked seven days per week with a total focus on that one goal.

When I left coaching to consult to business professionals, I was surprised by the lack of intensity in the business world. From what I saw, people just worked for the sake of working or to meet their financial needs, finishing and starting the day the same way over again. They lacked a daily passion and energy toward their goal, and there was lots of confusion about how to get from point A to point B (their goal).

The thing is, confusion is just randomness in motion. When it comes to getting where you want to go in life, I do not believe we are the feather being blown about by the wind, in random motion, taking off and landing on a whim. People who are living that way are chaotically trying things in fits and starts—and getting nowhere in the end. What's the antidote to this randomness? Flip the switch. By flipping the switch, we are creating a direct electrical signal that takes us from motivation to intensity and allows us to start and finish. By flipping the switch, we are activating an energy and drive toward a desired destination. We now have clarity. We now have direction. We now have high-value activity instead of low-value activity.

The amazing thing is that the switch is not just an energy thing. It's also a passion-filled driver that makes you want to be great and gives you the will to push for it over long cycles of time.

ACTIVATING YOUR WHOLE SELF

People ask me all the time, "Does everyone have a Prey Drive?" I, like Dr. Covey, believe that we were manufactured with "birthday gifts" that were given to us the day we were born.

Throughout our lives we seldom do the heavy work to find these gifts and utilize them, and instead we spend most of our lives unaware of them. Uncovering and using your birthday gifts is one of the most undertaught concepts in our society. Think of your own birthday gifts like this:

1. You have some unique talent that when utilized brings you to life with an energy and enthusiasm. There is an anticipation toward using your skills and talents.
2. This talent is rewarded in the market through recognition, affirmation, and money. You use your talent to solve a problem, and in exchange the world rewards you.
3. When you are in this talent zone, time loses all meaning, for hours and hours. You are in flow state and being rewarded at high levels by the marketplace.
4. You see yourself as an artist, athlete, or entertainer where your whole life can be built around your unique talent; it's where you get to "play" 80 to 90 percent of the time doing exactly what you love doing and are great at it.
5. This talent is typically at the intersection of your unique knowledge, impeccable skills, and burning desire and can be used to enhance another person's life or solve a problem.

In short, you are operating within your genius, using all your gifts, bringing your whole self to the process. When you are in your genius area, life becomes easier, and the mere ability to work daily in this area activates and reactivates your drive.

When I think of my birthday gifts and my genius, I have come to realize I love breaking down concepts so people can understand them. I love doing my thinking in inspirational places, like at our lodge that sits on 23 acres or at our house in Florida where my mind can run wild. I love taking concepts and turning them into "distribution channels," such as speaking, coaching, training, leading, publishing, and running boot camps. These are areas of monetization, where you can convert a problem into a money-generating activity.

Once you know what you love, what you are good at, what unique or neglected problems you solve, and what environments you aspire to be in, you can then structure your life around these passions. I call this "intentional congruence," where everything feeds your life in a healthy and positive manner.

I work hard to activate my drive daily through the four parts of my nature, which I learned from Dr. Covey:

Nurturing my *body* physically, typically by exercising.

Nourishing my *mind* by reading or watching something that stimulates me.

Tending to my *heart* emotionally by spending time in areas I am passionate about or with things that bring me joy.

Sustaining my *spirit* by feeding my faith. I typically do this by watching my favorite pastor in the morning so I'm deepening my faith and understandings at the same time.

The idea is to work on all four parts of my nature by 8 a.m. so that my Prey Drive is activated before I get to work. This is a routine I use daily to crank that engine to get ready to go into battle. We will talk more about daily actions in the next chapter.

THE PREY DRIVE IN THE STARS

If you talk to some of the greatest achievers in the world, from Tiger Woods to Oprah Winfrey to Michael Jordan to Warren Buffett, they'll describe some version of knowing they have a switch inside them—and then when turned on, it's what drives them. We all have that switch. We just need to find ours. When this switch is turned on, then every person, including you and me, becomes activated and ready to take action at a ridiculously higher level. It is at this level of alertness—when we are motivated, engaged, and, of course, driven—that we all perform our best.

Watch the miniseries called *Tiger* about Tiger Woods or *The Last Dance* documentary about the Chicago Bulls and Michael Jordan to see great examples of high-performing people learning how to activate their Prey Drive at high levels and under intense competition. It's not enough for these people to "peak up" one time. What makes them the greatest is their ability to peak up over and over again. It's their determination to practice at all hours of the night. It's their ability to deliver without fail. This shows the persistence and intensity they have that drives them to play at the highest levels multiple times over long cycles of time. This is what makes Nick Saban, the head football coach at the University of Alabama, so impressive—his ability to continue to win championships even when his top offensive and defensive coaches leave for other schools. His assistants come and go. He keeps winning.

If we were to pull back the curtain on all these people that we admire for their drive, we would see:

- Their Prey Drive is activated (typically by an external factor).

- Persistence is embedded in them (they have the ability to do the mundane with power).
- They have the intensity to pursue and keep pursuing (it's not capturing the prey that motivates; it's proving to people that they are the best).

All these people utilize the three core phases of Prey Drive to achieve extraordinary results. Not only do they activate the drive, but they continue to see the drive through to its conclusion, meaning they don't stop until they finish the job. Also, once the job is done, they have the persistence and intensity to come back and do it again and again and with even greater intensity. This is what separates them from the "one-hit wonders" who peak just one time. The fact that Floyd Mayweather, an undefeated boxing champion, could do it 50 times is what makes him so great in the eyes of so many.

The great sports psychologist Dr. Kevin Elko (I mentioned him earlier in the chapter) was once asked why he became a sports psychologist. He said at 18 years old he stumbled upon a book about sports psychology, and he went home that day and told his father he would become the sports psychologist to three Super Bowl teams, and he did. His vision was ignited. It stayed in his mind. This is brain science that capitalizes on motivation theory, which will be covered at length in the next chapter. Something has to be activated in your brain before you can amp up your physical energy and direct it toward a dominant aspiration. Notice how all these big-time people were exposed to some*one* or some*thing*. We could trace back each of these people's lives and see:

It was a coach.

It was a book.

It was an experience.

It was a stimulus.

For Coach Saban, his spark was and is the process toward perfection—and this next story illustrates what I love so much about him: Immediately following the final buzzer of one national championship win for the Alabama Crimson Tide, Coach Saban was asked by a reporter how he felt. I will never forget what he said: "I'm pissed off that those other college coaches have gotten a head start on me on recruiting."

This was less than a minute after being named the national champion, when his team was the *best*. How could you be "pissed off" in this minute? His mind had already begun to pursue a new championship. He was bored with the one he just won. Remember, in the wild, capturing the prey is not the reward for the animal. Pursuing the prey is what motivates the most. A dog gets most excited when it knows it "gets" to go hunting. The chase. The pursuit. The desire. The imagination. *The wantingness.* All these things come alive when you are pushing something *bigger* in life. Are you pushing toward something bigger in your life right now, or have you become bored and stagnant with your goals? Are you fascinated and motivated by something that activates your drive to want to pursue? Is there a hunger and enthusiasm being activated in you right now to expand toward something?

WHAT WE LEARNED AND WHAT'S NEXT

I'm a believer that until we "discover" our primary activator of our drive, we play at small levels. We take what life gives us, and we operate well below our potential. Progressing toward a worthy goal will motivate, activate, and reactivate your Prey Drive to keep pursuing versus sitting on the sideline and watching life go by. My hope is that this book is the catalyst for your drive and this chapter has prompted you to start thinking about your primary activator and the dedication over three phases it takes to get there.

Now we turn to look at some of the science of how I constructed this model of motivation and start moving you toward your desired outcome. The science that follows in Chapter 2 is based on qualitative evidence drawn from my experiences of coaching people for 30 years. I've tested the model with athletes, maximum security offenders, businesspeople, and students. In all of them there were things that activated and deactivated. The biggest revelation I had was the level of complacency that people experience when they get comfortable. This is why we have to stay in a state of doing, creating, and becoming, and never allow ourselves to stagnate.

 See where you *struggle* with the three phases of Prey Drive with this exercise and video with Coach Burt.

CHAPTER 2

The Science Behind What Activates You

If you are not willing to risk the usual,
you will have to settle for the ordinary.
—JIM ROHN

Have you ever caught yourself becoming lazy or complacent even when you know it's not good for you or your future? Do you have thoughts and dreams of what you can become but can't quite close the gap or activate your drive to achieve it? All of us reach lulls in our progress, become demotivated, or lose our drive for expansion, especially if we have been in the same game for a long period of time or we are in a game we feel we have mastered. For many, they can't get past the idea of moving, worrying about what it will take—the mechanics—to move toward their goals. Because they don't quite know how to move from where they are to where they want to be, they stay stuck, trapped where they are. My belief is that you should pick a target and move in that direction, and the mechanics will begin to take care of themselves with appropriate action. In this chapter we seek to understand why you get stuck, how to recognize when you are falling into this trap, and how to use the science behind some of the activators that can put you back on course.

At the time of this book's writing, I was coaching at least five people who were earning more than $2 million per year who were bored out of their minds and desperately wondered what's next. It's clear that just having money doesn't satisfy or fulfill, although it's better than having no money and feeling bored and unfulfilled. If money was the only thing that mattered, these people would be just fine, but they were antsy about what was next in their lives. They came to me because they knew deep down there was a greater potential inside them; there was a gap between where they were and what they were capable of achieving. This gap both motivates and frustrates. It's a great thing and a bad thing all at the same time, because it activates your drive but makes you feel like a failure since you can't quite get where you are going.

The Prey Drive is not about the money; it's about the pursuit of one's potential. Knowing that progress is a natural motivator of people, I believe we always need to be progressing toward something. This is why I like daily targets; so I know if I am moving in the right direction. I believe stagnation frustrates people because they are not progressing. Money goals can be the targets you choose to move toward, although this is just one metric of success.

When looking for trends around what activates or deactivates people, I learned that there are roughly 20 major motivational theories, all of which basically say the same thing: *we move toward things we want*—physiologically, biologically, and psychologically. When we're hungry, we move toward food. When we're thirsty, we find water. When we want companionship, we move toward people. But what happens when our needs are met? And do these needs change over time?

For most of us, we enter periods of stagnation. From my observations of the people I've coached on and off the court, this time of inactivity happens after a lofty goal is reached: a championship, a scholarship, a raise, a promotion, even moving into the next stage of a relationship. We want the things we don't have. It's human nature. But why does the passion have to wane? Why do people settle and decrease their wantingness? What I've concluded is this: that satisfied needs never motivate; only unsatisfied needs activate our drive.

If this is true, which I believe it is, the key to achieving a state of activation is to identify our needs and wants. Only then can we move into persistence and intensity. If you are trying to understand why you have become less than motivated, start by asking a simple question, "Do I want something more for my life, and am I willing to sacrifice or subordinate something in the short term to have it?

In motivational theory, when you get what you want, you become demotivated. Your Prey Drive is suppressed, which is why it's so hard for sports teams to win back to back championships. It's why shiny new toys wind up in a bin a week after a child's birthday. It's why people feel alone at the top. Psychoanalyst Sigmund Freud used the term "pleasure principle" to describe the theory that humans are hardwired to seek out pleasure and avoid pain, sometimes for immediate pleasure and gratification. Just like a baby spies a shiny new object and instinctively grabs for it, we want it, and we want it now! This hardwired need is the activation part of the Prey Drive. As we begin to mature and become disillusioned, we piece together that things worth achieving are somewhat out of our reach, and therefore require a ramp-up in our persistence and intensity to grab the object of our desire over time.

The word "passion" means "to suffer." So many people throw around the word "passion" that we forget it requires some unpleasurable things, like "cutting away" and sacrificing the immediate gratifications of the day-to-day. The lack of sacrifice is what disqualifies millions from getting what they really want, because they will not sacrifice the necessary things it takes to move toward their definitive ambition. It's the teenager who sacrifices attending the big house party in order to be fresh for the game the next morning. It's the parent who wakes up early on Sunday mornings, sacrificing an extra hour of sleep, to paint or write or finish a presentation, all before the family wakes up. Sacrifices of time, money, resources, relationships. In my opinion, a commitment is not a commitment unless it is backed up by the exchange of time, energy, or money.

EMBRACE THE SUCK: RETRAIN THE BRAIN TO SUSTAIN THE SACRIFICING

The brain is wired for one thing: survival through life-threatening uncomfortable things and conditions. The brain recognizes such threats and floods us with hormones that don't necessarily feel good but do come in handy to physically alert us and get us out of the swamp before the gators eat us. So we must teach the brain that when we are suffering for our goals, *we like it*. We thrive on it. There is an end in sight. Because if we don't do that, we can't keep the persistence levels we need. The Navy SEALs call this "Embrace the suck." Dabo Sweeney, the head coach at Clemson University football, calls it "Sucking the sour to get to the sweet."

One way you teach the brain how to thrive is to expose it to new ways of thinking, open it to new possibilities, and show it there could be a better way. In essence you gain "exposure" to something that you like and want more of. We see the power of exposure play out all the time: moving to a new place after holidaying there or picking a college major because of a group of mentors in the same field. Maybe you change your major after taking a riveting intro class in another domain.

I remember the first time I saw the speed and intensity of Miami, New York City, Los Angeles, and Chicago. It opened my eyes to a bigger world and a tremendous potential. I remember the first conferences I went to that exposed me to people who outperformed me. All of this activated a wantingness in me—to have more experiences and to outcompete others. Whether exposed to foods, music, culture, all the way to people and places, exposure is a powerful tool to initiate change and progress. Exposure implies that afterward a person is different, even by a little bit. Oliver Wendell Holmes once said, "A man's mind is stretched by a new idea or sensation, and never shrinks back to its former dimensions."

Lack of exposure is one reason people become complacent when they start making a certain amount of money. It's almost like being stuck at a "set point" similar to a set point in your weight, whereby your body will stay at the same weight until some sort of change occurs (e.g., sacrifice in the form of dieting). In this way, the mental set point, without the presence of an activator, brings us back to A, even if we had every intention of trying to get to B.

The science comes back to the Prey Drive needing to be activated by something that arouses your interest. A slight. A loss. An embarrassment. A competition. An exposure. An environment. A fear. A big target. A compliment and recognition.

A new game to play. Something has to embolden you to move toward something new. Something has to kick-start your wantingness. Just recently, for me, that something was simply an audiobook and a bigger way of thinking. Let me explain.

On a long car ride back from the mountains one weekend, I listened to the book *Super Founders*: *What Data Reveals About Billion-Dollar Startups* by Ali Tamaseb. The book breaks down the science and data behind those who start billion-dollar companies. Hearing the accounts of storied businesspeople activated my curiosity, creativity, and ingenuity—my Prey Drive. The flood of creativity that comes when in conversation with someone or when studying someone can activate that drive in you to want more or to have a new game to play. Think about yourself right now. Are you bored, stuck, complacent? Have you become casual or discontent with your current work? Has your Prey Drive gone dormant?

After listening to the audiobook, I initiated a call to two people who could help make my new business idea (my bigger way of thinking) happen. I made a decision to act. Ideas go from just ideas to income when you put a series of actions in place. You can't get caught up in the mechanics of how something will happen. In this case my new business idea went from a spark of an idea to a phone call to a potential new money-generating division in a matter of one car ride.

The enemy of the extraordinary life is the good life, so the strategy to find continued motivation is to tell yourself that you are "grateful but dissatisfied." Ed Mylett, one of the top thought leaders and a friend, calls this "blissfully discontented." You are grateful yet dissatisfied because you know there is another level for you. There is another gear. But you can't get a new result with an old preparation. To get a new result, you need a new preparation.

This desire for something new sets up tension in your life that propels you to constantly activate and reactivate your Prey Drive. The tension is a frustration between where you are and where you are capable of going. In our coaching programs, we call this A to B. For many, that tension comes from an outside factor that initiates an internal drive. Say, you know you need to lose weight, contribute at a higher level, earn more income, step into what you are supposed to become, or do what your conscience is telling you to do. The tension arises when something comes along and "alerts" you to this bigger future, opening your eyes to real possibility and creating a curiosity toward your bigger future. Something happens *to you* that triggers a movement and a new action. This is necessary for a new Prey Drive.

Change/motivation happens when there is enough "pain" or potential in your life, meaning you feel or experience pain or can visualize or see the potential if you take action. However, if the cost of change (i.e., the suffering and sacrifice of time, money, resources, relationships) is greater than the pain or potential, we merely stay where we are. This is because we are wired to avoid pain. We need to *hotwire* the wiring.

HOTWIRING THE SUBCONSCIOUS MIND

We know that the Prey Drive is activated by a want or desire, and that want or desire can be muted by the ideas of sacrifice and suffering. How, then, do we retrain our brains to embrace suffering, or as we discussed in Chapter 1, welcome fear, which is at the heart of why we don't want to suffer or "cut away"?

First, it's important to understand your subconscious mind and how it works. Tony Robbins, in his article "Reprogramming the Mind in Six Simple Steps," unpacks this. The subconscious mind is the part of the brain that is not in a state of awareness. It acts as a databank for your beliefs, previous experiences, memories, and skills. In the last chapter, we used the term "scripted," meaning that everything that you have seen, done, or thought informs your decision to act, guiding your actions. Your subconscious is also your guidance system. When people have limited experiences, meaning they are not exposed to new people, places, things, and ideas, they also have limited guidance in the area of potential. Think of it this way: When we have limited experiences, we have a limited scope of what our potential can become. Through exposure many times, our imagination is awakened, which could activate the Prey Drive to see a bigger vision and awaken us to a bigger future. If this vision is acted upon, we get feedback, either positive or negative, which could activate the drive to want more or less of something.

There are five specific things we can do to expose ourselves to a bigger future and actually reprogram our subconscious mind to see and act with this bigger future in mind. They include:

1. **FIND A CURIOSITY.** You are hungry to explore your potential and learn, so you go looking for something to lock into that both fascinates and motivates you. What is this for you? Move toward it with an action to learn more.

2. **GET IN AN ENVIRONMENT TO BE EXPOSED TO SOMETHING.** You seek out new information and are exposed to new ways of thinking and doing. This could be job-shadowing, listening to a great thinker at an event, or placing yourself in proximity to great people.

This is why you hear so many people talk about "getting in the room," as there is a higher level of intimacy when you are up close and personal learning something from the person who is most intimate with it.

3. **CULTIVATE AN AWARENESS.** You begin to recognize that there are certain times in your life when you are in a flow state and create uneven levels of action and intensity. What exactly is a flow state? A flow state is when you lose yourself in moments of positive energy, time loses all meaning, and you are inspired and creative. Very few in life get in a flow state. When you are in one, recognize it. Your awareness of this activation is critical to replicating it. Work to get back to an environment where you can sense it again.

4. **CREATE AN ACTION.** You begin to utilize an awareness to activate and reactivate your drive when you need it instead of sitting and waiting for some external factor to activate it. You learn how to flip the switch even when you have to create some external factor from nothing. I have learned how to change states of energy and quickly reactivate my drive when I'm in a funk. To spur action, you might create a competition in your mind, set a new target to achieve, or change your environment.

5. **GET FEEDBACK.** The market responds to your actions and serves as a feedback loop. Positive reinforcement feeds and reactivates your drive for more. In his book *The Art of Impossible,* Steven Kotler draws a correlation between this feedback and what happens inside the body when he says, "Positive attention from others causes the brain to release more dopamine than we get from passion alone. It also adds oxytocin to the

equation. The combination of dopamine and oxytocin rewards 'social interaction,' creating the feelings of trust and love that are so critical for our survival."[1]

In Chapter 4 we will deep-dive into the specific activators of your Prey Drive, but for now, let's look at some simple things you can begin to do today to activate and reactivate your drive:

1. **PICK AN AREA OF INTEREST AND CURIOSITY AND DIG IN.** Who is the top person in this space? What are you most interested in and fascinated by? Go online right now and book a conference for you to attend in the new year that can explode your growth. Don't get caught up in the mechanics of how something works. Find people who can and will inspire you to dream and think bigger. Which brings us to our next activator.

2. **GET IN THE ROOM WITH PEOPLE WHO ARE DOING WHAT YOU WANT TO BE DOING.** Shadow them; be exposed to their thinking; study under them. Right now, I'm looking for coaching and mentorship from people at the Harvard Business School, the top negotiators, and the best subconscious programmers in the world. I'm also being coached with my wife by Dave Blanchard, who owns the rights to all of Og Mandino's work on connection and equanimity. All of this is helping me activate what is already inside of me, but needed another person to help make it come to life. With Blanchard we are specifically working on connection, ways to handle anxiety, and strategies to go deeper with others.

3. **MAKE A NOTE OF ALL THE AREAS OF LIFE YOU ARE CURRENTLY DISSATISFIED WITH.** Draw up your ideal

outcomes in your mind. I call this exercise "From A to B." A is the current position, and B is the desired outcome. Every move we make should be one that moves us toward our B. You'll learn how to do this in the exercise that follows. "Finding Your B Game: Moving from Subconscious to Conscious." This one exercise could change everything for you if you commit to doing it daily until you have total clarity on where you are going in life and business. Allow a frustration to activate your drive to move toward a bigger future.

FINDING YOUR B GAME: MOVING FROM SUBCONSCIOUS TO CONSCIOUS

People wake up every day and take actions that have absolutely nothing to do with moving toward their goal or aspiration. Remember our simple concept of going from A (our current position in life) and moving toward B (our desired outcome). By writing down our next moves, ideas, and strategies with a system of action each night, we are actively telling our brain what we would like to externalize. In essence we are programming our subconscious mind to manifest a vision we see in our minds. The very exercise of coming up with a tangible outcome you would like to drive and envisioning the strategy to get there can activate your Prey Drive and begin moving you in the direction of your vision.

Here's how I do it. Each night, I sit down and write these things out:

1. My dominant monetized aspiration for my business this month in a tangible number that can be tracked and measured. This is typically a revenue number or a number of collections.

2. The biggest opportunities available to me that I need to be focused on that would move me closer to my B (we call these "Level 10 opportunities"). Think of big opportunities you need to follow up on, get involved with, or focus on that can really move the needle in your life.

3. The most powerful people I know who can help connect me, offer counsel, or open doors toward the B (we call these people "Blue Marlins" because a blue marlin is a big fish versus a little fish).

4. The people who are closest to making a decision to move forward with me so I can invite them to take an action (we call this our "Red Zone," which is a football term indicating you are on the 20-yard line and close to scoring).

5. Ideas on money generation. This week I wrote down a marketing plan to market one of my biggest boot camps by using an eight-week mentoring cycle combined with the actual event to bundle and stack the value. This one strategy could generate $180,000 in new revenue. Think big opportunities for monetization by using your skills and talents to solve big problems for others. I like to remind people that money changes hands when problems are solved, so selling really is just going out into the marketplace and solving problems for others. See how quickly you can take an idea and turn it into an action that solves a problem for another person. Once I have the idea, I focus on the action I want

people to take. I then find a big problem I believe they would pay to solve. I then create a concept that would attract people to the idea. I invite them to something in the future to learn more about how I can help them (strategy session, webinar, in-person event). At the event, I offer them the ability to move forward with me to master the skill that solves the problem.

By spending time with myself and my thoughts, I actively engineer ideas and strategies that would move me closer to the B (the ideal outcome). This nightly exercise identifies key actions to take and tells the subconscious mind that this is where we are going. The next step is turning thoughts into actions. I devote a minimum of two hours per day toward actualizing the preceding steps. The Prey Drive has to be activated daily to take the intention and translate it into action; otherwise your brain will literally just sit there and wait for you to tell it what to do.

So why do people sit with their thoughts and not act? You could say that the answer lies in Newton's first law of motion: "An object at rest will stay at rest unless acted on by an outside force."

1. They don't have a system for placing their thoughts.
2. They don't have a clear B, or they haven't taken the time to define it or understand the importance of it. (You would be shocked at how many people do not have clarity of B.)
3. They are satisfied with their current position in life; therefore, there is no Prey Drive activation.
4. They have become lazy or don't care.
5. They are afraid of something. Fear should be used as an activator of the Prey Drive, not something that suppresses it.

We've discussed many reasons for not going for one's B: fear, lack of exposure, lack of programming, and so on. Now remind yourself that all these things might feel distressing, and then tell yourself you like this feeling of discomfort. Or at least tell yourself you aren't afraid of a little sacrifice or discomfort or uncertainty. You know it leads you places.

Next consider the things that make you feel resistant to activation. Most likely you are confused. Remember, confusion is randomness in motion, and the way to rein in randomness is by controlling it with clarity, tangibility, and measurability.

Think of yourself at position A. If your life were a map, A is where the words "You are here" are printed. This is your current position in life, with all the things that you may or may not like about your current position. You could be and are most likely frustrated and/or dissatisfied with this position, or at least facets of your current position. You have a desire to move toward some outcome in the future. Let's call that outcome "B." When you imprint the vision in your subconscious mind that you want to manifest outcome B, your brain begins to work toward that vision with an intention. The B must be clear, tangible, and measurable versus vague.

This means that that the subconscious mind needs very specific direction on what it's working toward. It's not enough, for instance, to say you want to go to Europe. Tell me where? What part, what city, for how long, and why? What do you want the smells to be like, the interactions, the tastes? Do you want to accomplish something there, even if that is "to do nothing"? Being this specific and writing down your targets weekly and even nightly will ensure your goals remain clear, tangible, and measurable, so you can then imprint the vision for B in your brain and activate your Prey Drive to achieve it.

Here are some examples of how I ensure that my vision for my B game is always clear, tangible, and measurable:

- **I AM CREATING $10 MILLION** in revenue for my company. (This is the revenue target I would like to drive for the company of top-line revenue.)
- **BROKEN DOWN**, this is $833,333.33 per month, $250,000 per week, and $41,666.67 per day for a five-day workweek. (This is a breakdown of the big goal into monthly and quarterly targets.)
- **TO GET TO THIS NUMBER**, I am taking 35–45 specific actions—which we call "high-value activities"—with a specific frequency over a specific time frame. (This goes back to mapping out the daily actions I will take to create or realize the numbers I have created. The high-value activities are specific money-generating activities.)
- **I WILL HAVE 1,000 PEOPLE** in Monster Producer, my coaching program. (This is the coaching program that would be considered the "core product." It feeds the other programs and solves the problem of structured revenue production.)
- **I AM WRITING** a bestselling book called *Flip the Switch*. (Thank you for purchasing it and helping this dream come to life.)
- **I AM BECOMING AN INTERNATIONAL THOUGHT LEADER**, just like my greatest mentors and especially my primary mentor, Dr. Stephen Covey. (This is a qualitative goal I set when I was 31 due to the impact Dr. Covey had on me.[2] It's hard to measure unless we look at revenue, books sold, or people reached. In essence it gives me a blueprint and path to follow in an aspirational way.)

- **I WILL HAVE 50 GREATNESS FACTORIES** around the world, which are unique and inspired locations where people can work, create, learn, and activate their potential, complete with shared office space, permanent office space, auditoriums, and podcast studios. (We are building the first one in downtown Nashville, with plans for expansion around the world.)
- **I AM RAISING $100 MILLION** to build Greatness Factories around the world. (To build the Greatness Factories around the world, we need capital. Action steps would be (1) to find those who specialize in raising large amounts of capital and are experienced in starting and replicating something in multiple locations, (2) to spend time with people who have built something similar, and (3) to build the dream team to bring the dream to fruition.)

Now take a few moments to write down where you are now—your A. Be clear, tangible, and measurable. Use time frames, financial amounts, people's names, and so on. The reason for this is that our brains can't tell the difference between things real or imagined. The more detailed you are and the more measured, the more real your brain detects things to be. This helps your brain build new pathways, and new pathways mean new habits.

Next draw up the B for your life. Be specific and detailed. For instance, you don't want to say, "I want to get a promotion." You want to say, "I am earning $250,000 per year doing exactly what I love doing, which is _____." Don't say, "I want to write a book." Say, "I want to write a historical novel that takes place during the time of the Gold Rush and that will be published by a major publisher."

I have done this A to B exercise as many as 65 times in a 30-day cycle because I believe in its power so strongly. You see, each day I'm programming and reprogramming my subconscious mind as I create my ideal life based on the new information, breakthroughs, guidance, and strategies I'm learning daily. I'm telling my brain what is going to happen. Typically I'm increasing my goals and seeing clearer paths to move from my A to my B. It's amazing to me when I write down that I need this person and within six months the person shows up in my life. I believe it is the power of manifestation, and it is available to all of us who intentionally sit and cocreate our lives with vision and action. I can't tell you how many B goals I have created that have actually manifested. Remember, I didn't get caught up in the mechanics of how I was going to make it happen. I placed it into the universe through intention and began taking action toward it.

I have to call out one point before we keep moving: it's important that you actually *make your goal something doable*. The last thing you want is to set a lofty goal that is out of your control and might frustrate you more than activate you. Sometimes we set ourselves up to fail when we don't start with what's doable. For instance, you might really want to train for a marathon, but with small kids at home, it might be impossible for you to find babysitting or to leave them alone for several hours on the days for those long runs. So commit to several 5Ks instead, or condition yourself on a treadmill instead of having to leave the house. The point is, keep your eye on the goal, but don't let the goal be so out of reach it's not doable for you.

Getting with the Program

First, for this exercise, get out an old-fashioned pencil and paper, because the use of motor skills and the ability to carry the paper around with you are all part of the campaign to program your brain. Next, nix the following words from your mind: "I can't," "We won't," and "It can't be done." The brain tends to remember negative words more so than the positive, so think of them as words that threaten to cause a short (or a total blackout) when you try to flip the switch.

Complete the following statements with as much description as possible:

"MY POINT A LOOKS LIKE": (E.g., "I'm overworked and underpaid." "I'm working in a job I hate." "I am yo-yo dieting and unhealthier than ever." "My family feels disconnected." "I like my company but want more.") These are typically areas of life you are currently dissatisfied with.

_____

_____

_____

"MY POINT B LOOKS LIKE": (E.g., "I want to work less without worrying about the bills." "I need to change careers completely. "I want to lose weight." "I want to feel more connected with my family." "I'd love to be more recognized by my boss." "I want to work from X and enjoy being in a creative state doing what I love doing up to 80 percent of my time with a team and structure around me that I enjoy working with.")

_____

_____

_____

NOW DESCRIBE WHAT YOUR POINT B LOOKS LIKE BY BEING CLEAR, TANGIBLE, AND MEASURABLE: (E.g., "I want to not have to bring my work home on weekends." "I want to leave engineering and become a nurse." "I want to be the weight I was on my last birthday." "I want to play a board game with the kids just like I did when they were smaller." "I want to have a conversation with my boss to tell her I want more challenges.") The key here is to specify tangible goals and to think of things that bring you joy and happiness.

_____

_____

_____

"WHAT ACTIVATED ME TO WANT TO GO FROM A TO B?" (E.g., are you feeling competitive with someone else? Are you concerned about making enough money? Are you energized by an idea you heard a colleague talk about? Or perhaps you're not on speaking terms with a family member, or someone didn't recognize you at a reunion because of your extra weight.) Remember the activators of the Prey Drive here, as they motivate this desire to move from A to B.

_____

_____

_____

"THE ACTIONS I NEED TO TAKE TO GET ME FROM A TO B ARE": (As examples, you might research night schools and the costs of nursing programs, cut out sugary drinks and take the stairs, have a family game night, email your boss immediately and set up a meeting.) The concept of mental mapping is critical since you need to go there in the mind before you go there in the body. This is why sitting down at night with a notepad and writing things out is so important. It confirms in your mind your next step of action.

_____

_____

_____

"ARE MY CURRENT ACTIONS ALIGNED WITH WHAT NEEDS TO TAKE ME TO B?" IF YES, WHAT ARE THOSE ACTIONS. IF NO, HOW ARE THE ACTIONS NOT ALIGNED? (E.g., are you cutting out soda but drinking wine with friends? Are you emailing but not pressing "Send"? Are you bringing up past conversations during family game night and causing tension?) Review your B to determine which actions are not aligned—look for those that waste time. When people take actions that waste large amounts of time, it is because their B is not clear enough, is not big enough, or does not matter enough.

_____

_____

_____

"WOULD I DESCRIBE MY ACTIONS AS LOW-VALUE ACTIVITIES OR HIGH-VALUE ACTIVITIES? WHICH ONES ARE LOW, AND WHICH ONES ARE HIGH?" (A low-value activity is any activity that you participate in that moves you *away* from achieving your B. An example would be writing a list of foods for the week and leaving it on the counter. High would be meal prepping for the week.) Write out all the things you participate in that have nothing to do with your B. These are low-value activities, and most waste large amount of time in drama, worry, or lack of execution. Stay focused on taking actions that create energy toward the B. An example would be forging key relationships with people who can take you further, faster.

_____

_____

_____

"AM I AWARE OF MY POINT B? IF I AM UNSURE, WHAT DO I WANT?" (Tap into that desire, the pleasure principle that makes you excited to grab the shiny object or achievement. Think of a B that will both motivate and fascinate and that is big enough to get you excited to move toward. What comes to mind? For example, "I want to be validated." "I want a million dollars." "I want to be loved and feel safe." "I want fame." "I want to feel balanced in my work and life.") Create both tangible and intangible outcomes you wish to drive here that matter to you.

_____

_____

_____

"TO GET WHAT I WANT, WHAT WILL I NEED TO SACRIFICE? TIME, MONEY, RESOURCES, RELATIONSHIPS?" (E.g., "At first I'll need to work weekends in order to make room for school at night." "I'll need to hear some negative things from those I love to move past our rift.") A commitment is not a commitment if you are not willing to sacrifice time, energy, or money and put resources into it. You most likely will have to sacrifice something to get something better in the future in the areas of knowledge, skills, desire, confidence, and/or relationships. By focusing on who can help you, instead of how you can work the mechanics, you most likely will need to pay the money to get in the room with the right people—those who have the knowledge and relationships you need for advancement. They are the ones who can help advance you toward your dreams. I spend most of my time asking this question of who is qualified to solve a problem for me rather than beating my head against the wall trying to figure out the answer myself.

_____

_____

_____

"DOES THIS SUFFERING FEEL LIKE IT WOULD OUTWEIGH THE POTENTIAL GAIN?" (E.g., "I will give up an extra hour of sleep in the morning to start a cycle of building discipline in the body, mind, heart, and spirit with morning workouts." "I will sacrifice an extra hour of phone calls to hit the targets I set.") Remember the concepts of "sucking the sour to get to the sweet" and "embracing the suck." The outcomes will be worth the sacrifice. For me it is a welcome bargain you make with yourself: suffering in exchange for achieving your goal. It could be making sales calls you don't enjoy so you can increase your sales. Or maybe it is going to the gym to get the body you want. There will be something you have to give up to get something new. This is the way life works. People want the diet pill, but they don't want the diet. Just remember that the process is just as important as the product. Learn to love the process.

_____

_____

_____

"WHAT IS MY TIMELINE FOR THE GOAL? WHY THIS TIMELINE?" (E.g., "I have a 30-day cycle to hit my monthly revenue targets that I will break down into weekly and daily goals. I will track that goal daily with a tracking system and recalibrate when needed. This will give me a goal, a timeline, and a tracking mechanism.") While you may be able to get some short-term wins quickly, I believe in the power of daily habits over long cycles of time to build the muscle and make it automatic. Many people can start in 90-day increments, but most struggle week to week to keep a commitment and see it through. I recommend setting a target with a deadline such as "I will lose 20 pounds in 90 days." Then break that goal down to 30-day increments and daily goals so you can absorb each win and make the bigger goal feel more attainable. Remember, for you to commit, the outcome will have to be bigger than the sacrifice.

_____

_____

_____

"WHAT DAILY ACTIONS DO I NEED TO TAKE ON TO MAKE SURE I MEET THE TIMELINE?" (E.g., "I need to get enough sleep every night." "I need to make contact with my network on this matter at least twice a week." "I need to stay positive and expect I will meet roadblocks." "I need to refresh my math skills before I take the entrance exam.") The key ingredients here will be knowledge, skill, desire, confidence, and relationship. These are the five things that can move you toward an outcome.

_____

_____

_____

I cannot stress enough that this journaling needs to be done daily. Make use of that eraser on that good ole No. 2 pencil, and revamp, replan, rewrite, and keep rewriting so you keep rewiring your brain so you will never have regrets. As you move through your days and weeks, trial and error will inform your next steps; but as long as you decide to keep cutting away what doesn't work and making room for what does, you are staying in the activation stage of the Prey Drive. Now, fully activated, you can learn to persist and intensify.

WHAT WE LEARNED AND WHAT'S NEXT

There is a power in you that is clear about what you want, how you are going to get it, and what actions you will take daily to manifest it. The A to B is an easy concept to use to tell your brain where you are going. The mental mapping outlines the strategy. *Remember, your brain works for you.* You don't work for it. Tell it daily to thrive versus survive, and give it instruction on where you want it to go. The first step is getting clear on where you are going. The A to B exercise initiates and activates the Prey Drive to move toward your B, toward something that matters to you.

Don't get caught up in the mechanics. Use the creativity of the Prey Drive to start taking one action at a time. Initiate and follow up until you begin to see concepts through to their logical conclusions. This dreaming period is one of the most exciting parts of the Prey Drive and activates the imagination in fun and creative ways. It's exciting to see what you come up with on your A to B journey.

In the next chapter, we discuss the next step, finding your purpose—or more accurately, letting your purpose find you.

 Find your *primary* activator of your Prey Drive in this quiz and video with Coach Burt.

CHAPTER 3

Screw Your Why

How to Let Your Purpose Find You

It is not enough to be industrious; so are the ants.
What are you industrious about?
—HENRY DAVID THOREAU

Nothing deactivates the Prey Drive more than waking up every day and spending a large amount of time doing something you are not engaged with, do not believe in, or feel like you have already mastered. Much of what keeps people frustrated and deactivated is being unable to find their talents and abilities and distribute those abilities in a meaningful way to help others.

I believe work can become the distribution channel for your unique talents, but first those talents and abilities must be found and then refined. Then they can be marketed and distributed to the world. They become your purpose. Think of it this way: you exchange your abilities and skills for the opportunity to help others advance in some way. Many times, people will pay for this exchange because you guide them toward a bigger future. In essence, people pay you for your past. Your past helps them build their future.

The way we spend time is excruciating to observe. I was once at a training course many years ago, and the instructor, whose name fails me, offered these statistics, which have stuck with me all this time. The average person will spend:

23 years of life sleeping

9½ years in cars

6 years eating

15–25 years getting an education

35–50 years working

Notice how many years you will spend working as opposed to doing everything else. To wake up and do something that you are not supposed to be doing would waste a large percentage of your life and, I believe, would create regret at some point in the future. A Gallup poll taken in July 2021 indicated that roughly 20 percent of people are engaged with their work, and most others struggle to find their talents and distribute those talents through their work at high levels. What results is their becoming frustrated and irritated much of the time, knowing they are not doing what they were hardwired to do. It is precisely for this reason that people buy books like *Flipping the Switch*, attend seminars, and hire coaches to help them bring clarity to their confusion. They know on a fundamental level that if they engaged in Jeff Bezos's regret minimization framework (see the

Introduction), they'd be let down by their choices in life by the time they were 80 years old.

We can prevent regret by exploring our talents and spending time working harder to match those talents with the correct work for us. It's never too late.

Flattened, unenthusiastic professionals have a plethora of books to choose from to help them find their business mojo. One of the most popular approaches is to find one's "why." The idea, and a popular approach for many, is if you find your why, even in the things you don't want to do, you will succeed and be fulfilled. Another way of saying this is if you find your purpose and live your values, life will get better. However you prefer to phrase this, I'm not knocking it; and I have much respect for Simon Sinek, who made "why" a popular theory. The way he packages his thoughts and ideas is brilliant. I just happen to disagree with starting with why. I think you should just start and keep going *until your purpose finds you.*

I understand the thinking. Find your purpose, and life takes off. Find your purpose, and you'll do something big. You will have motivation and drive and energy toward something. This implies that you need to dig down deep and find your true motivation of *why* you do what you do. Until you find your why, your life will lack purpose and just won't be that impactful or meaningful. This sounds logical in theory . . .

Except after coaching for more than 30 years, I've seen people get up and do remarkable things every single day without knowing their why. Instead of mulling over their purpose, these people make it their business to pursue things that interest them until they have a revelation that they are in their true strength zone. Once in that zone, they match their talents with their work, and the world begins to reward them with love, appreciation, and money.

This is the reason, during my panels, I surprise people when I tell them, "Screw your why." And I usually get some tentative applause and cheers.

Later, people approach me and say, "Thank you for saying that. I felt so dumb and stuck because I hadn't found my why in life."

This one concept both liberates and paralyzes millions of people around the world daily. Some literally just sit and wait for this revelation to take place in life, and it never does. The why is in the doing, in the acting, in the movement. You won't find it by sitting and waiting.

So it is not really the person finding the purpose—the why; it's creating a life that invites purpose to find the person. This happens when you take action and move toward things you are curious about and are interested in. It happens through action. The Prey Drive is the instinct to pursue. You pursue your talents. You pursue your potential. You pursue things that bring you joy and happiness. You pursue relationships. You pursue opportunity. I believe it is in this pursuit where your purpose begins to find you versus you find it. It is in these moments—when you are doing what you love doing, doing things you are talented at, and solving a problem or adding value to another—that you have a revelation that this could be your purpose.

CREATING CONDITIONS FOR YOUR PREY DRIVE TO THRIVE

How do we get to that state where there is an alignment between your talents and the distribution channel you utilize for those talents that refuels your drive?

Over a cycle of time (the persistence of the Prey Drive) is when you refine a skill and the world begins to reward you in the form of love, affirmation, reputation, referrals, and ultimately money. And the money exchanged for your effort is in direct proportion to the strength of your skill set and the size of the problem. I believe the most skilled and talented people have a higher earning power because they are using their unique skills to solve big problems.

And while you might not have found your ultimate why, you are still being paid and acknowledged for your skill, which supports a cycle of confidence, curiosity, more skill acquisitions, more feedback in the form of money and accolades, and repeat. It is the process of trying something, getting and responding to feedback, and feeling fulfilled that helps you realize if this is a unique skill you possess and a problem you want to solve. This process essentially becomes your purpose.

I like to define purpose in this way:

- The use of your "unique talent" in the world to solve a problem for another, a process you enjoy
- The distribution of your unique skills and talents
- The use of your talent to help others in exchange for fulfillment
- The fundamental relationship between your talent/skill and someone else's problem

When I set out to help other people find their purpose, I start with these definitions. Notice the use of your talent to help solve a problem in exchange for fulfillment. I believe it is in this exchange that you begin to locate not only your abilities but your purpose. This only happens when the Prey Drive is activated to pursue your unique talents and abilities. Think about big problems you are uniquely qualified to solve based on your own demonstrated capacity for solving these problems for yourself.

Also notice the definition about distributing your unique skills and talents. Remember, work could be a distribution channel for your talents, and when your talent is strong enough and your skills are superior, you get rewarded at a much higher level. When you distribute your talents to the world to solve big problems or bring new opportunities to people, you make yourself eligible for bigger payouts from the world.

BECOME A DOER, NOT A TALKER

There is an age-old argument about whether talent is hardwired or is developed through our early scripting in life. Regardless of the answer, there is a gap between those that *achieve* and those that *talk about achieving*. In the social media world, many who don't do anything convince the public they are doing a lot. This is why I say you should check out the people who are doing the helping. Be wary if you find:

It's the out-of-shape doctor giving you health advice.

It's the broke financial advisor teaching you how to invest.

It's the coach making the average $47,000 per year that's teaching you how to build your business.

These examples are definitely talkers, not doers!

You want to be a doer. I think your purpose finds you when you are actively pursuing something. It never finds you when you are static, whining, or not taking an action. What action could you take right now in the direction of a dream you have?

What relationships could you be cultivating? What can you put on the schedule to pull you toward something in the future? Whom do you need to be studying under to learn the skill you need to advance toward your ideal scenario?

Each day, my mind is attracted to all kinds of ideas and is stimulated by exposure to others. This activates me to want to take an action. And when I do take an action and get positive feedback, I want more because it feels good. That's an external factor, like the ones discussed in Chapter 1. When we are pursuing something, our Prey Drive is activated. We are hunting and gathering. When we are stagnant, confused, or not moving in any direction, our Prey Drive is deactivated.

It's important to note that it's impossible to take action on every idea. Remember in the last chapter, we talked about making our goals doable. Recognize this and think about problems that you see every day that you are uniquely qualified to solve with your talents. These are "recurring problems"—they continue to come up and nobody seems to be solving them. This is a great opportunity for you to capitalize on by using your talent and purpose to solve a big problem in the world or a problem for a certain group of people. Think about someone you are motivated by that is doing something you secretly wish you were doing. Think about an area of life that you are fascinated with. Think about a problem you would be passionate about solving. Think about the last time you were involved with something that really flipped your switch and you really enjoyed it.

I didn't know I wanted to be a coach until I started coaching, but I immediately fell in love with the planning, the development of strategy, and the thrill of the game. I didn't know I would enjoy coaching adults until I coached adults after writing my first book. I didn't sit down, find my why, find my purpose, and then go out into the world and do something. *My purpose found me because I took action.* That's the disagreement I have with people that think you have to find your why before you do something big in the world.

Purpose and the Curiosity Ripple Effect

I believe that being curious creates a ripple effect that sets conditions for our purpose to find us, instead of our wasting precious and limited time in search of something we might not know—or ever know—on the surface. So what can we do not to waste our time? Well . . .

1. **PURSUE A CURIOSITY.** This is an interest in something you have that prompts you to want to learn more. For me at 15 it was coaching. At 25 it was writing. At 35 it was marketing and promotion. At 45 it's passive income and real estate. I study, seek out new info, and go looking for ways to combine these curiosities into meaningful ways that ultimately could be monetized.

2. **HAVE A "REVELATION" THAT YOU ARE BOTH GOOD AT AND ENJOY DOING.** My definition of a revelation is a sudden dramatic moment where we instantly realize something. One revelation is when we lose time while doing something. We realize afterward that we were so engaged, so in flow, our talents took over to lead us to a positive energy exchange. Other revelations can be in the form of positive feedback or solving a problem. Many times, while exchanging your talent for taking on and solving problems in the world, you discover something (you have a *revelation!*), and that something could be your purpose.

3. **IDENTIFY A SKILL THAT YOU ENJOY AND ARE GOOD AT AND THEN PACKAGE AND MARKET IT.** Can you take that talent you are now aware of and package it? Can you create something the consumer can feel, touch, taste, or see? Take your talent, and put it into a tangible form that another person can consume.

4. **LOOK FOR WAYS TO MONETIZE YOUR TALENT.** Monetization is the exchange of money for talent. So many people have a problem with this. When they enjoy something or have a talent, people tend to take that for granted and say things like, "I couldn't possibly charge you for that." If we can't charge for what Dr. Stephen Covey calls our innate "birthday gifts," then what can we charge for? Allow monetization to take place (should you want it to) doing what you are good at and enjoy.

5. **INVESTIGATE WAYS TO USE YOUR TALENT TO SOLVE PROBLEMS IN THE WORLD.** *That's* your purpose. Purpose is found in trying various ways to utilize a talent and in getting feedback from the marketplace that you are in the right lane. In my lifetime of writing 17 books and speaking around the world, my best ideas have always originated in market feedback. In the process of this pursuit of learning and doing, I believe there will be moments where your purpose grabs you and says, "This is it." You are now taking what you love doing and what you are good at doing and marrying those factors with a need in the world that you are uniquely qualified to solve.

Curiosity necessitates action and pursuit. So it's not surprising that curiosity can activate your Prey Drive.

Pique Your Curiosity: Questions to Consider

Grab that pencil and pad again, and write down your answers:

1. **WHAT INTERESTS YOU?** Looking back on my coaching career in athletics, I was always fascinated and motivated by "inner-engineering" the players to build a competitive intelligence. I was fascinated by the psychology of taking a team toward a defining ambition like a championship. Now I love studying successful people and big concepts and deconstructing those concepts to help others find their talents and abilities and activate their drive. What both fascinates and motivates you?

    _____

    _____

    _____

2. **COMPLETE THIS SENTENCE:** I've always wanted to learn (or try):

    _____

    _____

    _____

    The reason for this is:

    _____

    _____

    _____

3. **WHAT COULD YOU STUDY FOR HOURS ON TOP OF HOURS THAT YOU LOVE DOING?** For instance, when you have free time, where does your mind go to learn about something? This is activation. One way I like to ask this question is, "If I handed you an iPad and told you that you had three hours to study anything you wanted, what would you choose? What interests you? If I gave you a free ticket to any conference in the world or paid for you to spend time with one person that you are fascinated by, who would that person be, and what would you go to learn?" My wife loves design, real estate, and hospitality. She watches home editing shows, and real estate shows so she can activate her mind—which ultimately ends up in expensive remodeling projects. I push her to "monetize" her talents by combining her eye for design with real estate and hospitality. One way we do this is through our retreats, where I do the coaching and she handles the design of the experience and the hospitality.

_____

_____

_____

FROM CURIOSITY TO MASTERY

Now that you understand that a why isn't necessary to get started, let's break down a cycle you can use to warm up your purpose. Doing so allows you to step into and become aware of what your true purpose could be. This is part of the ripple effect we spoke of earlier—of taking action, getting feedback, and moving toward something we are interested in.

- **IT ALL STARTS WITH *A CURIOSITY.*** It's 16-year-old Bill Clinton meeting John F. Kennedy. It's Elon Musk reading comics as a kid and saying, "In the comics, it always seems like they are trying to save the world. It seemed like one should try to make the world a better place because the inverse makes no sense."
- **CURIOSITY IS THEN FOLLOWED UP BY AN *ACTION.*** You study something; you follow up on something; you get access to someone; you sit at the foot of a master. You initiate an action toward something that you are interested in.
- **THAT ACTION CREATES A *FEEDBACK LOOP.*** You say to yourself, "I like this" or "I hate this." You are turned on or turned off, which causes you to repeat the action or move on to something else.
- **YOU THEN *DETERMINE* THAT YOU *ENJOY* THIS AND WANT TO CONTINUE.** This has piqued your interest.
- **YOU BEGIN AN *"INNOCENT CLIMB"*** with humility of working the muscle and developing a "hard skill," which I refer to as a "primary skill."
- **THIS SKILL GETS *BETTER AND BETTER*** with the second part of the Prey Drive, which is persistence. People begin to notice.
- **THE SKILL BEGINS TO BUILD *DEMAND* FROM OTHERS.** This initiates monetization of the talent.
- **YOU BEGIN TO BECOME *KNOWN* FOR YOUR SKILLS AND FOR OVERDELIVERING,** prompting you to develop "networks of people" who want this skill and tell others

about it and your excellent service, multiplying the demand.

- **THE FEEDBACK GETS *STRONGER*,** and the Prey Drive is activated over and over again, prompting you toward mastery.
- **THE NETWORKS OF PEOPLE YOU OVERDELIVER FOR INTRODUCE YOU TO *NEW ASSOCIATIONS*,** driving up your "person of interest score." This brings you more and more people who are interested in your talent and skill.
- **YOU FIGURE OUT WAYS TO *SCALE* THIS TO HIGHER LEVELS,** driving up the monetization and your personal wealth.
- **YOU WORK IN THIS PURPOSE FOR LONG CYCLES OF TIME UNTIL YOU ACHIEVE *MASTERY*** and become one of the greatest.

ACTIVATING YOUR PREY DRIVE IS GOOD FOR YOUR HEALTH AND YOUR CAREER

The amount of time and emotional energy that is eaten away trying to psyche yourself up to do something that is not in alignment with your true talents is mind-boggling and energy-zapping. Quite frankly, it's exhausting. Imagine a world where you wake up and spend 80 to 90 percent of your time doing what you love doing with people you love doing it with and generating healthy profits doing it. The entertainer performs. The athlete plays. The artist draws. What are you supposed to be doing, and is it in alignment with what you are currently doing?

There are also serious psychological penalties when you are not playing in your strength zone from a biological standpoint. In his book *The Art of Impossible*, Steven Kotler writes, "We are all aligned for optimal performance. This is how the system wants to work and there are serious consequences for trying to buck the system. Both disconnection from meaningful values and disconnection from meaningful work are major causes of anxiety and depression."[1]

I estimate from my experiences that 9 out of 10 people are on the wrong bus—they are doing the wrong things and are totally misaligned with their talent and work. I believe work serves as the distribution channel for your talents, and when in alignment, you get into this flow state that Kotler writes about, which is "optimal performance."

The next step is to build your life and your business around your talent so that you are literally "playing" daily in your primary skill area and getting paid for it. Think of the artists who get to sing their songs to thousands at a concert or the athletes who get to play a sport for millions of dollars. When you pay to watch them perform, you are actually paying to watch them work. How much would someone pay to watch you work right now based on the quality of your skill and the size of problem it solves for others? Add the feedback from the market and get better and better, refining your purpose even more. After the long journey in the same direction, you begin to become "world class," and this is when you graduate from the minors to the majors, especially regarding compensation.

I don't believe money buys you freedom. *I believe skills buy you freedom.* The stronger the skills you have, the more money you are going to make. When you can utilize the money you make from the skills you have to better your life and the life of your family and to pursue bigger and bigger goals, your Prey Drive is activated over and over again.

I was 42 and had been coaching since I was 15 when I think my purpose finally found me, or at least I now had a way to intimately know it and now define it for others. This clarity is vital to your being appropriately compensated in the market and to truly know what your purpose is and how to utilize that purpose. I had been successful in the various realms I had entered but still struggled to uncover this purpose, having a hard time to articulate it when asked. When I made an association between the term "Prey Drive" and what I had been doing since I was 15, I stumbled upon what my life's work really was: it was to use my unique talents to unlock a drive in people—a drive that had been latent or undeveloped. It combined my skills of deconstructing a concept and translating the concept to an audience. I could take a complicated idea and make it simple and then deliver it with a cadence and rhythm that unlocked something inside another person. I quickly discovered that I could utilize this talent with people all over the world. Think hard right now about when the market rewards you in the form of love, recognition, or referrals.

If you're a person who feels paralyzed by not knowing your why, it's OK. Take an action toward something that interests you. Pursue a curiosity. Study various things. Try different avenues. Get around other people whom you find interesting and who can awaken something inside you. Engage in dialogue with others. Do the work so that you are moving and not stagnant. Right now I guarantee you are curious about *something*. . . . So take an action right now to get involved with that something to see if it sparks an interest in you.

My guess is that your purpose will find you when you are taking these actions and are growing your awareness. As I write this book, I'm watching and observing my wife pursuing various things, and my guess is that her purpose is about to find her and she's 40. I can see the interest, the curiosity, and the action. The market will give her the feedback she needs, and her internal feedback will help her decide if this is her purpose or not. If she persists and works the muscle in her talent areas, that talent will expand and begin to help more and more people. When homed in on a specific thing, she has a total focus and intensity in that area. This is the Prey Drive at its finest, being utilized to attack a potential.

WHAT WE LEARNED AND WHAT'S NEXT

Purpose never finds people who are stuck, static, or in a rut. It finds those who are dynamic, engaged, and curious about their potential. Opportunity follows energy. Opportunity follows movement. Opportunity follows action.

I'm letting you out of the "why" trap to know you have a bigger future. When in doubt, take an action. Your why will find you.

In the next chapter we dig into the five main drivers of the Prey Drive so you can begin to see what it is that flips your switch.

 Answer four questions to have your *purpose find you* versus *you finding it*. . . . in this video with **Coach Burt.**

CHAPTER 4

The Five Activators of Your Prey Drive

Creating Conditions Aligned with Your Uniqueness

Every person who has ever lived has had a Unique Ability though most people haven't been conscious of it. Because of this lack of awareness, most people haven't experienced the infinite rewards that come from being able to harness and develop their natural talents and pursue their passions wholeheartedly.

—DAN SULLIVAN, CREATOR AND
FOUNDER OF STRATEGIC COACH

In 2009, Garrett Camp grew frustrated by the lack of consistent, quality, and friendly taxi service in San Francisco and wanted to decrease the cost of direct transportation to and from various destinations. Camp, a computer programmer and founder of StumbleUpon, was frustrated by an external factor—poor taxi service—that activated his Prey Drive. He imagined a taxi service that could be summoned with the click of a button on one's smartphone. Camp partnered with Travis Kalanick, who founded Red Swoosh, a file-sharing company that he sold for $19 million. And together the two men would go on to create a company called Uber, which now boasts more than 101 million users and has transformed the transportation industry forever.

You have ideas like this. Sparks of inspiration that occur in reaction to a problem you consistently see. As I noted earlier in the book, I refer to these as "recurring problems"—problems that people complain about but never do anything about or problems that never seem to be resolved. Based on your unique past and your unique experiences, you may be uniquely qualified to solve a certain problem but may never act on your instinct, or maybe you start and never finish. How many of us have seen a new product or service and have said, "I should've thought of that!"? Or maybe you did, but you didn't do anything about it.

The Prey Drive is activated by external factors. In Camp's case, he was tired of accepting inconsistent service and wanted to create something that would solve this problem. He engaged in the other two phases of the Prey Drive, *persistence* (he contacted people who could help him) and *intensity* because he followed up the activation moment with the fierceness needed to take an idea and see it through to its conclusion (in this case creating a new service). Kalanick had the intensity and focus to bring the discipline and business know-how to fight through the adversities and opposition to bring Uber to the market. (See the documentary on Showtime called *Super Pumped*, based on the book *Super Pumped*, to know more.)

If you are a quick start by nature, you may come up with great ideas but lack the follow-through to see those ideas to their conclusion. The action, consistency, and discipline to weather the storms, handle the conflict, and move an idea into mainstream is what is impressive, especially in Uber's case. The amount of resistance alone that the company has faced from local governments and the entire taxi industry, which was resistance to its new disruptor and competitor, would be enough to make a lot of people quit. But not when the Prey Drive is in charge. Uber's story is the ultimate display of the Prey Drive in its true form.

In Chapter 2, we touched upon what external factors activate our Prey Drive. We also have discussed the conditions necessary to make sure those factors are initiated. From early scripting to exposure, we can learn to call on this drive when needed. Becoming acutely aware of the things that activate us, being specific, and then utilizing them is critical to our future success. Yes, we want to be curious, we want to be persistent and intense, but those things cannot occur if we first do not see the opportunity for activation. This chapter is designed to help you become much more aware of whether you react (without thought and impulsively) or respond (pointedly and thoughtfully) when an external factor "threatens" you. Only then can you use the science of the Prey Drive to reprogram your brain to turn typical deactivators into activators.

As a reminder, the five activators of the Prey Drive are fear, competition, environment, embarrassment, and exposure. While this chapter will help you determine your primary activator, I believe that you are most likely motivated by all five drivers at different times and in different ways, so you might have a primary and secondary activator of your drive. Steven Kotler in *The Art of Impossible* said, "Since impossible is always an arduous trek, elite-level performers never rely on a single source of fuel to sustain them along the way."[1] Similarly, I believe you "stack" these Prey Drive activators on top of each other as I did during the pandemic. When fear of loss (my primary driver) combined with competition, exposure, and embarrassment (my secondary drivers), I found that freakish level of persistence and intensity that helped me outperform that year.

Remember, emotion is not fueled by passion. Real emotion is fueled by conflict. This is why many times your Prey Drive is activated by real conflict that initiates a deep survival mechanism inside you that you just can't reach until provoked. The loss of the Prey Drive is typically the loss of the fight in you for something, which is why people become complacent and mediocre. They have lost that fight, that deep survival to pursue and protect. When people lose the urge to fight, you can watch their progress gradually decline.

The idea is to not avoid these conflicts. That's unrealistic. They will always exist. It's knowing how to turn them around that opens the opportunities for activation. On a plane ride back from a brutal speaking engagement where I struggled to connect to the audience and met great resistance, I had to fight hard against letting the conflict win. I had to make sure I didn't go the route of blaming or whining. So I wrote a list on a yellow notepad and titled it, "Tired of Messing Around List." I thought about the things I knew I spent more time talking about than doing. I was ready to burn the ships and never go back. In that moment the conflict fueled me to want a new life, to have a better experience, and to no longer tolerate a level of mediocrity I had been accepting from myself and those around me.

Take a minute right now and write down your Tired of Messing Around List. To figure out what messing around means to you, revisit some of the concepts we've discussed thus far. For instance, consider whether you are talking about things but not doing them; not taking accountability for failures; not engaging in curiosity; not considering your skills; not exposing yourself to people, places, and things; or partaking in negative self-talk ("I can't," "I won't," or "never").

TIRED OF MESSING AROUND LIST

_____

_____

_____

_____

_____

_____

_____

_____

Now that we got that out of the way and you're no longer messing around, let's look at the five primary activators and do the heavy lifting to find yours. Finding and knowing your primary activator and how to call on it when needed is the equivalent of superheroes calling on their superpower when it's necessary to level up. I'm not saying you can live 100 percent in this state, but at certain times you need to know how to amp it up for maximum impact and to get the new results you're seeking.

THE FIVE ACTIVATORS OF THE PREY DRIVE

Activator #1: Fear

Fear: An emotion created by a belief that someone or something is going to harm us in the future. We either face everything and rise or face everything and run.

Sounds like the fear most of us grew up with, right? What if I don't buy that definition? What if I reject that definition? What if I oppose that definition? I believe fear to be a positive emotion that is absolutely necessary to activate something deep inside you to achieve a freakish level of success. You already know that I think fear can be our friend, not our enemy. When you change how you see what you see, in this case what fear is, you can now use fear as fuel versus a paralyzer. Fear poses a choice. Either you can "face everything and run," or you can "face everything and rise." Eliminating much of the paralyzing fear and anxiety people deal with is critical to achieving a much higher degree of success and impact.

Fear is universal and can activate a person's drive. It's the response to fear that makes the difference. For example, confident people with a high Prey Drive convert fear into fuel. Fear is their friend. When they are afraid of something, they switch to another gear. They push out. People who lack confidence typically "contract" when they are afraid.

Maybe you identify with fear as an activator, but you need to go deeper. Not all fear is created equal. Certainly, one can be afraid of a thunderstorm but much more afraid of driving in the thunderstorm. Jimmy Evans, one of my favorite pastors, talks about the difference between pit bull fear and poodle fear. Pit bull fear is real. Poodle fear is imaginary or small.

There are many ways fear can show up in your life, including fear of loss, rejection, failing, retaliation, or attack. Then there are the fears of losing money, losing your lifestyle, and losing respect. There is also the fear of being unmasked as a fraud, which is often coupled with the fear of being laughed at.

Because I was a basketball coach early in my life, I put an enormous amount of time into preparing and planning for the games and scouting my opponents. I spent almost three hours per day just planning practice because I wanted to win so badly and didn't want to waste one second of precious practice time. Upon reflection, it wasn't the winning that drove me; it was the embarrassment and fear of losing. The fear of being average or getting beaten prompted me to work and rework my plans over and over and over. It forced me to pay close attention to small details. This prompted me to never allow myself to get complacent and relax on a past win. This "use of fear" shows up every day in my coaching business. Because of the fear of loss I experienced as a basketball coach, I now know how to prepare and never allow complacency to creep in.

Winning on Tuesday night only to lose on Friday night taught me a valuable lesson: I don't care about the success I had yesterday. In the business world, what takes years to build up can take seconds to tear down. Those who grow complacent believing times will always be good will end up losing big at some point in the future. Remember Sigmund Freud's pleasure principle from Chapter 2? Trying to bring people always to play like they are an underdog or behind is a tough sell, but wantingness as an activator works.

To train the brain to embrace fear, we need to tell ourselves how much we are comfortable with fear. Here are some mantras I've developed or collected over my career, thanks to my experiences on and off the court:

- We go to bed tired and we wake up hungry.
- Today doesn't care about yesterday's success.
- There comes a time when winter asks what you did all spring and summer.
- It all goes to zero at midnight.
- What takes years to build up can take seconds to tear down.

To repeat what I said earlier, in the business world, yesterday's wins can quickly become today's losses if you get too comfortable. The satisfied salesperson who had great sales last month becomes the complacent salesperson this month. He stops working the selling system. He stops engaging with his clients. He stops going 7 to 15 touches in his follow-up. He stops doing everything that made him successful because he has lost his fear. God gave the Israelites just enough food to make it through the day so they would have to forage again the next day. You need the same mindset.

FEAR OF . . .

Here are some of the fears I see that people face that can be used as activators.

Fear of rejection. At 25 years old I went through a terrible breakup. I bought and returned an engagement ring I had purchased for the person I thought I was supposed to marry. I went through six months of clinical depression, lost every bit of my confidence, and realized that in my relationship, I had placed all my previous confidence in another person's hands. As a result, I felt dejected and believed I had messed up the best relationship of my life. I felt incredibly rejected.

As I worked my way back out of all those internal feelings, I made up my mind that I would never allow another person to control my confidence again (see more about that in my book *SWAG*). During this time, with the help of a great friend, I would come to an incredible revelation—that *you don't have to live with rejection.* Some will want what you have; some won't. So what. People are not rejecting you when they choose someone else. They are merely saying they prefer something else.

So remove this internal fear of rejection that prohibits an external action in you. Many will never make a phone call, work a strategic partnership, or try to put a bigger deal together due this one simple fear. Reframe your view of the situation, and use it to spur you on.

If you felt you were rejected by someone in your past and you experience this "hint" of rejection, I encourage you to use that feeling to activate a drive in you. Allow the emotion, the pain, and the past to drive you toward this bigger play you are capable of. To avoid this feeling of rejection, make up your mind that you are the buyer, not the seller. You have the buying power to work with whom you want to because you are a person of value. If others do not see that value, then keep moving to those who do. I like to use the feeling of rejection to activate something inside me to prove others wrong, to rise to the occasion, and to create extraordinary results that possibly I could not have gotten if I hadn't sensed that feeling in the first place.

Fear of failing. I hear this one a lot. This has a lot to do with how you define "failing." In life, you are going to win some and lose some, but when you listen to your "instinct," the Prey Drive in you, you win more than you lose. Combined with the regret minimization formula that Jeff Bezos spoke of (see the Introduction) where you ask yourself, "Will I regret this in the future?" there really is no failure. You don't lose; you just learn. Keep in mind the Einstein quote, "I'm not so smart. It's just that I stay with problems longer." Successful people view failure as part of the process of succeeding. They do not define themselves as failures when they make mistakes. Each mistake gets you closer and closer to your defining ambition. Mistakes are necessary to move you forward.

Fear of success. This one shocks me a little, but it's a fear many people have. Oftentimes this is experienced on a subconscious level. People who are afraid of success are typically self-sabotagers. A self-sabotager is the one who stops dead in the tracks of success. The person who starts gaining weight back eight pounds from goal weight. The person who decides not to go for the promotion. The teen who applies only to "safety schools." Possibly these people fear the burden that will come with the responsibility of having success in life and of having to continue that success. I believe success breeds success. While there is an increase in responsibility, there is also an increase in the impact you can make and experience.

Fear of losing everything. This is a real driver. If you have built a great life and put years of blood, sweat, and sacrifice into something, you certainly don't want to lose it. You should wake up every day with a healthy fear that your current lifestyle can be lost if you don't continue to do the hard work. One bad decision. One exposure of risk. One thing can come along and knock down everything that you've built for years. Fear of losing everything is my primary activator of my Prey Drive. This, along with setting targets so big that I don't have margin for wasted days, keeps me on my game. This is the coach in me that says, "If we lose one game, it could turn into a losing streak, so let's not lose that one." This one activator could be the propelling force you need to build the persistence and intensity you need to do big things in the world.

Fear of change. One of the greatest detriments to the activation of the Prey Drive is the unwillingness to be open to new ideas. This is a result of a fixed mindset that prohibits the Prey Drive to be activated by exposure. People who have a fear of change won't get in the room to learn a new philosophy to better themselves or be open to an idea that could enhance their lives. Because of this overwhelming fear in their lives, they never open new doors or get new results. To them, it's too anxiety-provoking to learn anything new. In this case, exposure to learning is actually an activator of their Prey Drive. This continual cycle of learning and growing increases their skill sets, setting them up to expand in their lives.

FEAR IS YOUR PRIMARY ACTIVATOR IF:

1. You sense you are losing something; as a result, you find another gear (meaning you step it up a notch).
2. You feel rejected or "not good enough," and that triggers you to find another gear.
3. You think you are going to lose something that is valuable to you, and so you find another gear.
4. Losing respect, position, authority, or something that matters to you lights a fire under you to find a way to make it work.

Another gear could indicate a heightened performance level, a new intensity, a deeper persistence, or a much higher level than your normal performance level. You might experience a spike or jump in your numbers or outputs.

Activator #2: Competition

Competition: A game to play, a trophy to win, and something to pursue

Tilman Fertitta, the Texas billionaire who owns over 600 restaurants and the Houston Rockets, is a straight-talking business guy who believes that "business is sport." I agree. Activating a competitive spirit in your people and in yourself is vital to doing something big in the world. As a basketball coach, I learned to hate losing more than I loved winning. It was a competition. It was a game to play and look forward to. But that's sports, not public speaking. You wouldn't expect speaking professionally to spark a competitive edge in someone, but if you put speaking side by side with a sport, you can see parallels:

There is a time compression.

There is something to win (an audience).

There is a scorecard. (What did we sell?)

There is pressure and anxiety.

These goalposts help me increase my game, spurring me to reach for a high level, especially when the goalposts move with a new audience, a new location, a new message. I specifically love when the lineup is full of well-known and famous people, and I'm the underdog.

David Goggins, ultramarathon runner, ultra-distance cyclist, triathlete, public speaker, and retired US Navy SEAL and author of *Can't Hurt Me*, talks about having a trophy case in your mind and not on a shelf in your bookcase. This trophy case in your mind represents a set of mental wins you can track and measure in the inventory of your mind versus physical trophies we won as kids that we put on our shelves and that ultimately end up in some storage unit. A mental win could be to set something in the future and achieve it, or it might be to take business and turn it into sport.

Your mental win could be a real competition that you are vying for. On the other hand, part of the battle for many is they don't have a game to play or a championship to win. There is nothing in their future that prompts them to practice and refine their skills and test them in the marketplace. If this is the case, it could be an imagined competition with another person who has no idea you are competing. In either instance, the purpose is to activate or reactivate the Prey Drive. This competition could stimulate you to take an action, create something in the future, or enhance your skill set somehow. By placing something in the future that you want to win, you'll want to practice, role-play, and allow the experience to become the test to see how well you did. In sports, practicing and role playing through simulation is common. In the business world, it is uncommon. I believe this to be the reason so many people merely repeat the patterns of the past, because they do not receive any feedback on how to improve or get a new result.

The greats have something to win. They practice and simulate. They role-play and work through various scenarios that could occur. They test themselves before they go into battle. Even the best Top Gun fighter pilots in the world fly only 45 minutes per day, spending most of their time in practice, role play, and simulation testing so they are ready to execute when called upon. When there is competition or something to earn, there is potential progress toward a goal. There is something to win. There is a need to practice, role-play, and test, because this refinement increases the probability of achieving a desired result.

If there are no scores to tell you whether you're winning or losing, if there are no key performance indicators, revenue targets, or benchmarks, if there are no stats that show growth, how can you expect to be motivated? Without benchmarks for success, you'll just make it through each day. You'll clock in and clock out without anything being meaningful. Where there is no scoreboard, there is no measurement of success.

I set daily targets on revenue. I set daily targets on touches, follow-ups, and scorecards. I take my big goal (my B) and break it down into 30-day increments and then weekly increments and then daily increments. The goal is to *win the day*. When I win the day and build momentum (which is just energy headed in a direction), I begin to win the week. I've made up my mind that my positive energy is going to be greater than any negative energy I face in a day.

ARE YOU VYING?

One synonym for "competing" is "vying." You are vying to capture something in the future. You are vying to be the best in the world. You are vying to show people that you are the real deal.

The average person wakes up, repeats what he did last week, and doesn't have any idea if he is winning or losing. That's not vying. But the cycle can be broken with targets, which will create a new cycle of confidence, purpose, and productivity that activates the Prey Drive. To move from treading to vying, answer the following questions:

- **DO YOU HAVE TARGETS** that are quantifiable, meaning you can measure them, and are you working toward them daily? I have daily sales targets, overall yearly sales targets, and big goals I want my company to hit. I have financial targets and daily checkpoints with a system to achieve those targets. If you don't have quantifiable targets, you might want to start with a goal that you can measure in the future.
- **HOW DID YOU DECIDE** what your targets would be? There is no science behind how I set targets, but I have an awareness of what I think is possible. I set aggressive financial targets and then try and reverse-engineer how to get there.
- **WHAT ARE YOU TRYING TO WIN?** For instance, it can be a new deal, a revised target, or the B that you are moving toward. Or it may be recognition you want or a goal you desire to achieve.

- **WHO IS YOUR GREATEST COMPETITOR** you should be learning from who is kicking your butt? Choose someone in that industry who is achieving at a high level, and model what that person is doing.
- **DOES THE PRESSURE AND DESIRE TO WIN** (or not to lose) activate you? This gets into three of the five activators of the Prey Drive: competition, environment, and exposure. It is important to know how you perform under pressure. Are you ready to handle the pressure that could come along with producing at a higher level, or do you pull back under pressure?
- **WHO IS THE BIGGEST PERSON** in your industry that you should be competing against today?

If you believe you are not vying or winning the day, consider the following:

- Did you compete every day?
- Did you prospect like you should?
- Are you failing to generate multiple flows of income, meaning are you missing your financial targets because you are too dependent on too few strategies or too few income streams or sources?
- Are you using various strategies to find and fill market needs?
- How many products do you currently offer, and how many are generating profit?
- Are you engaging with your client base as you should be?
- Are you marketing and promoting like crazy?

The competition isn't beating you. You are beating you. Most people have what are called "internal problems." These internal problems deal with insecurities that prohibit them from advancing. Sometimes I refer to these as "considerations," which are internal thoughts that prohibit external actions. The following are some of the most common roadblocks I see as a coach:

- Inertia
- Fear
- Your tiny thinking
- Your past
- Your own considerations
- Your potential

Look at your "Tired of Messing Around List," and add some of these to it, if you haven't already. You must first have a desire to win, to produce, and to find a way, or you will never be competitive. Take some pride in showing up early, staying late, getting the job done, hitting your numbers, and being a market leader. Don't compete against some local person. Compete against the best person in the world.

Before I began my speech as the keynote speaker at an insurance rewards banquet, the CEO asked me to "wake the people up and push the agents hard." I'm always up for a good locker room talk that forces a person to either step up or get out, so I pushed hard and challenged the agents. The inertia was so strong and the complacency so obvious that when I pushed the agents to compete, they didn't even have a response. I pushed them by challenging them to expand and grow. I pushed them with a framework that would cause them to do some deep inner work. I pushed them with a strong message and coaching methodology. Their response? Nothing—no energy, no passion, no frustration.

They just sat and looked at me. They didn't even get fighting mad. They just sat there and accepted their performance with no emotion at all. The CEO had wanted me to push them with a strong message to see if we could activate their Prey Drive. The culture was so cemented and the mindsets so fixed that they were not responsive. This indicated that this message was new to them or the culture was so apathetic that something dynamic would not help. It was malaise across the board. It was something I had seen only a few times in my 30 years of coaching at that level. This explained to me that their insurance agency was stuck in old ways of thinking, and as a result, only a few in the room actually had a desire for expansion. Most did not want an accountability structure or an external motivator, such as a coach, stimulating them. They resisted the stimulus to grow.

I pointed to the number one agent who had just won all the awards, and I asked him to stand up in front of the crowd of almost 300. I said, "Congratulations for winning the number one spot in your company."

He smiled until I said this: "These people are not the ones you should be competing against though. You've won this award multiple times, right? There is no one in the room clearly good enough to beat you. Who is the number one agent in your state? What about your region? What about the United States? What about planet Earth? Whoever it is, that is who you should be competing against."

Consider whether your personal culture might need some competition, and if so . . .

- Quit comparing down and start comparing up.
- Decide if it should be you versus the best.

- Decide if it should be you versus your potential.
- Decide if it should be you versus some real challenge you are trying to win.
- Set a competition in your life. Set a target. Set a goal. Work on a new skill. Go and win the trophy in your mind to show *you* that you can do it. Don't allow yourself to run out of purpose.

COMPETITION IS YOUR PRIMARY ACTIVATOR IF:

1. You hate losing more than you love winning. (That was me as a basketball coach, but more than anything it had to do more with the embarrassment of losing.) Many who are motivated this way are called "defensive pessimists"—they keep their expectations on the lower side as a means of helping them prepare for the worst. In the lead-up to a given event or situation, they tend to mentally rehearse all the ways things could go wrong.
2. You need competition to get motivated and are always looking for people to compete against, even when they don't know there is a competition.
3. You need a worthy opponent, a real nemesis, to play your best—someone who engages you in competition daily to help battle-test you to get to a new level. Without a nemesis, you don't push like you need to, and you can't reach deep inside you for that competitive fire that most likely came out when you were afraid of something.

4. You become lazy and complacent when there is no real competition. This happens many times when people become the best in their company and lose their desire to become the best in the world.
5. You want the recognition that comes with the win. The real competition is with yourself, but you want others to recognize how good you really are.

Activator #3: Environment

Environment: An environment of inspiration or expectation that causes us to play at a higher level versus a lower level

Environments are healthy and habitable when there is a balance of accountability, inspiration, and creativity. Your environment for your Prey Drive to exist is no different. Certain conditions and certain elements must be present in order for your Prey Drive to activate. Part of creating an environment is setting the expectations of that environment. Accountability is another. We all go to different places with different people at different times for different reasons. We have certain expectations of Disney World that won't match up with the ones in the CrossFit gym or your church.

Expectations have several different purposes. For example, can you imagine these environments without structure or accountability?

Can you imagine the military without any expectations?

Can you imagine top sports teams making everything "voluntary?"

Can you imagine Olympic coaches telling world-class athletes that it doesn't matter when they show up or how hard they practice, nor do they need to strive for maximum potential?

Can you imagine an industry where there is no accountability? No structure? No targets?

These are among the thousands of ways an environment can inspire you to play up or play down. Without an environment that causes you to perform at a higher level, you contract to a place of comfort. Remember, it's human nature to seek comfort and safety. Very few people have the persistence to push themselves without the help of an outside stimulus.

You need people in your life—such as a coach, leader, mentor, or manager—who expect something from you. These people expect you to show up. They expect you to be prepared. They expect you to plan your days. They expect you to follow through. They expect you to take an extraordinary level of action.

As a championship high school basketball coach, I worked hard to create an environment of expectation. Our vision and goals were outlined from the beginning of the season. There were expectations and consequences. There was positive peer pressure. There was tracking, and with it there was accountability. There was a system of both personal and professional growth that we followed. It was disciplined and produced results. More than anything else, it produced an environment of excellence in everything we did.

There are feelings that certain environments evoke that can activate one's Prey Drive. For example, I remember certain environments that actually scared my players. Some did not perform well because they had a feeling of pressure, tension, and even hostility. The environment evoked either a fight response or a flight response. One (fight) activated the desire to get in the arena and go at it. One (flight) activated the desire to contract or run. When you were the visiting team playing certain teams, the fans yelled, clapped, screamed, and wanted to punish you. It was a tough environment. This environment crushed some of my teams, including the ones not talented enough or tough enough to fight through their discomfort. But for some of them, the environment forced the maximum outputs of their talent and potential. They played the best games of their lives.

One of my favorite players of all time, Anne Marie Lanning, scored 43 points one night against the Eaglettes because the environment reminded her that she had something to prove, something to pursue, and a trophy to win (in her mind and on her shelf). When we played weak teams, many times my players underperformed due to the competition. We may have won on the scoreboard but lost in the game versus our potential. Does winning matter when you know you play weak competitors and don't have to exert any force toward your potential?

From time to time I host musical events at an 8,000-square-foot lodge in Tennessee, where we do corporate events and retreats. The concept of the musical nights is a way to network with other top players while enjoying top musical entertainment you would most likely hear only in major venues. These nights are special, as we get to see major artists distribute their talents to the world in an intimate setting.

For our last event we had a rising star named Lewis Brice perform. The younger brother of major artist Lee Brice, Lewis was a joy to watch. His energy combined with his talent and enthusiasm convinced me he was on his way to stardom. We also brought a good friend named Wes Cook in to play. As a career musician who most likely had grown bored with playing on Broadway each night to an audience of tourists coming from around the world, Wes brought a new level of energy and excitement to his performance. Deep into his set I went on stage and said, "I want to see Lewis and Wes play together." Both stepped up their games and sang their hearts out. The creativeness of the environment and the inspiration they got from each other activated the Prey Drive in both to find another gear. When you're in the room with people distributing their talents at the highest levels with top levels of commitment and dedication to their craft, you have no choice to put up or shut up. Getting in the right environment will force you to play up or get out, and this is exactly what most people need in order to play up.

The goal here is to *create an environment* in which you can thrive. Some need pressure environments. Some need creative environments. Others need environments where there is accountability, direction, or consistency, and still others need to be in a home office. What you want to avoid is being in an environment where you don't have to perform and are allowed to just goof off. Too many people take the path of least resistance. This means taking or finding the easiest job, or working for a manager who is disengaged or doesn't care, or taking large amounts of time off during which you do nothing or waste it doing a low-value activity.

Take a moment right now and think about the environments in which you perform at the highest levels, and ask yourself why you are not placing yourself in those environments weekly. The following questions are a great place to start:

- Look at the coaching programs you are involved in. Are they elevating your life toward your B and potentially activating your Prey Drive? Some programs inspire, and some teach. I believe you need a combination of both.
- Look at the culture at your office. Does it foster an environment in which you are improving and maximizing your potential? Is this where your unique talents should reside?
- Look at the expectations you are placing on yourself and others in relation to your outcomes or performance versus a standard measurement. How do you measure up compared with the top people in your company? How do you measure up compared with the world that you compete against?
- Look at your physical self. Are you reaching your physical goals? Are you in an environment where you can thrive physically? Do you have physical goals that you are activating to achieve so you are operating at a maximum level of confidence in this area of life?
- Look at your financial goals. Is your financial advisor the best person for you? Are you in alignment with your ideal financial targets, and are you in alignment with your long-term wealth plans? Is your passive income greater than your living expenses, and are you hitting your financial targets you set for yourself?

As you work through these questions and think about what environments are most supportive for you, you may realize that it's time for an upgrade in every area of your life. If so, let's get to work so you can place yourself in a position to prosper.

WHAT KIND OF ENVIRONMENTS WILL CREATE A GREATNESS FACTORY FOR YOU?

It's crucial that you understand the types of environments you personally thrive in. For instance, I work out harder when I'm in a gym with others around me than I do working out at home. I'm much more creative in quiet environments, where I can read and concentrate on my thoughts and come up with ideas alone. When I work in the energy of a big city, the movement and circulation of people activate my drive for a bigger think, faster action, and an overall creativity that I love.

Most people thrive in different types of environments depending on what their goal or task is. Start thinking through where you do your best work for everything you want to accomplish. Knowing this will help you produce the best outcomes. Think through the following questions to get those answers:

- Where do you feel the most relaxed?
- Where do you feel the most creative?
- Where do you feel inspired to take action?
- Where do you feel reflective?
- Where do you feel inspired to slow down and reevaluate?
- Do you work better by yourself, or are you stoked by the energy of others around you?
- Do you work well autonomously, or do you need guidance and leadership direction?

- Do you need to be in a competitive environment, or can you create your own competitions?

It's also important to realize that environments are so much more than the physical space. Environments are vessels for coaching, structure, expectations, a scoreboard, and leaders who expect an outcome and take pride in that outcome.

If your work environment is filled with distractions, low-value activities, and little or no expectations, you need to make a change. So many people get up daily and go to environments where there is little or no energy, no expectations, and no concept of winning or losing. These types of environments typically have no consequences either—but the reality is, where there are no consequences, there are no changes of behavior.

If you find yourself in these types of environments, it's time to reevaluate and possibly make a serious change. I believe environments are critical to maximizing your talents, optimizing your potential, and staying in creation mode—all of which will result in you producing maximum outputs.

ENVIRONMENT IS YOUR PRIMARY ACTIVATOR IF:

1. You need the right environment in order to play at a much higher level and feed off that environment.
2. You cannot focus on your own or push through if you are not in the right environment.
3. When placed in the right environment, you produce at freakish levels.

Activator #4: Embarrassment

Embarrassment: A feeling of underperformance when measuring your current production against what you believe you are truly capable of

While speaking at Grant Cardone's 10X Growth Conference at Mandalay Bay in Las Vegas, I thought I did a great job of communicating my message. I had a rhythm and a cadence to the message. The audience of 10,000 people seemed to resonate well with what I was saying. But after speaking and doing around $250,000 in total revenue sales of my products and services, within the first hour of speaking Grant Cardone came up to me and said this: "You've got to get better at your pitch. Russel Brunson just did $3.5 million."

I felt embarrassed by my own performance, and after that day I began to study how the best in the world pitched their services. I now fully understand how important your pitch is to a quality presentation. Sure, I can still do much better in this area and am working on it weekly, but I improved dramatically because I was embarrassed. And while most would think this embarrassment was a bad thing, it was far from that. It was a great thing because it activated my Prey Drive.

When you're personally embarrassed by how you performed or what you've currently done with your life in comparison with what you're capable of doing, this can be a very strong driver.

Salespeople are often embarrassed by their own performance versus the performance of other team members. Sometimes we're financially embarrassed. We may be embarrassed by the car we drive or the house we live in. But there's a key part of this embarrassment we need to realize—this isn't about being embarrassed *in comparison* with others around you; it's about being embarrassed because you know you can do better in your life. You know there's more under the hood.

That being said, I do not personally embarrass people when I'm coaching, but I will ask the hard questions that makes them think about their performance, such as:

- Help me understand why you have so much potential and are performing at such a low level?
- Help me understand why I see so much potential in you, but you don't exert force and energy into that potential?
- Help me understand why you are consistently at the bottom of the food chain?
- Help me understand why you are playing at such a local level when you should be playing at a national level?

Too many people begin to justify their performance by comparing it with that of their peers. They say things like, "I'm number one in my company." "I'm doing better than all my friends and family." "I'm the best at what I do."

Here's my philosophy: someone should always play at a higher level, and you must find that person and compare up. Without the exposure to something bigger, we continually live in the world of "false positive," where we tell ourselves that we are better than what we are. You should learn to be personally embarrassed when you don't maximize your potential.

Think of areas right now in your life that you might be embarrassed by:

- The house you live in
- The money you are "stacking away" instead of investing
- The quality of time you spend with your family, kids, or passions

- The amount of money you give to charity
- The level of income you have versus what you are capable of earning
- The car you drive in comparison with what you could be driving
- The size of your company now in relation to what you believe it could be
- The person you are now compared with the person you believe you are capable of becoming
- Your feelings of jealousy toward others
- The fact that your letting yourself down or your lack of commitment to your goals
- An inability to see things through to their conclusion

The idea is to turn your embarrassments into inspirations. There are lots of theories about comparing yourself with others. I use others as a baseline. For instance, say I am running a coaching company and doing $X million in revenue, but another coaching company is doing $Y million in revenue. I use that knowledge to see what I could be doing better, as I believe there is always something we can do better. The goal is not to live in the gap of where we are in relationship to where we could be, as this produces lots of frustration. Instead we should utilize the success of others to activate our imagination on what is possible for us. I believe this is a healthy way to utilize what may feel like embarrassment.

One exercise I use on a routine basis is this: Look at the top industry leaders in your space. What are they doing that you are not doing? What strategies could you borrow from them? If I placed you side by side with those leaders, what would be the difference between you and them? What are they doing that you are not doing? Where would your gaps be? Here are three ways you can find some answers:

1. Spend time studying the top 1 percent of performers in your space, and write down the things they are currently doing that you are not doing. Don't get caught up in the mechanics of this or the cost of this, but begin by asking, "What is my version of this?"

2. Take a look at your current strategies and the outcomes of those strategies, and begin by asking if these strategies are working or if they need to be retooled.

3. Pick one person you really admire and respect, and see how you can get in the room with that person to observe how the person operates. By observing and measuring your progress versus the other person's, you may activate your Prey Drive for expansion, and you can see exactly what you need to do to enhance your performance. Many years ago, I went to a Tony Robbins event with one intention, to see how he got 10,000 people in a room. By focused observation, within 15 minutes I was able to determine how he did it, and it gave me what I needed to expand my audiences.

In addition, look inward for what makes you different and where you can win. Each of us has a different background and different experiences, and these differences help us differentiate us from our peers and competitors.

EMBARRASSMENT IS YOUR PRIMARY ACTIVATOR IF:

1. You use your feelings of embarrassment to do better, play harder, or perform at a higher level or to stretch your current capacities to new levels.
2. You constantly utilize the anger you feel when others have prospered more than you have to activate a drive inside you to catch up and surpass them. Instead of being envious toward them, turn your envy into action.
3. You find yourself in rooms where your confidence is *low* and other people's confidence is *high*, and you feel inferior. Use this real or imagined "inferiority complex" to spur you into action to produce at a higher level. You get in the right rooms. You go to the right conferences. You expand in new ways.

Activator #5: Exposure

Exposure: Seeing or experiencing something that activates the imagination to dream bigger and take bigger actions

Exposure activates curiosity. You've seen something new, something exciting, something that opens up your brain to new possibilities. You have now been exposed to something you didn't even know existed, like a better life, a better way to do something, a better philosophy. It's like someone from the country going to a big city for the first time. If you've never been to New York City, you don't even know the energy of it. But when you go, now you know. Now you understand. Now you think bigger. You go home and think differently. Your mind has been expanded. Your boundaries have been broadened.

Growing up in a small town, we didn't travel the world. In fact, many years we vacationed in the same place, Gatlinburg, Tennessee. It is beautiful with mountains, rides for kids, and even Dollywood. There is *nothing wrong* with Gatlinburg; actually, I love it. But there is a bigger world out there. I remember when I first got on a plane. I remember the first time I saw the speed of New York City, or ate the pizza in Chicago, or felt the energy of Miami. I was hooked on wanting to be part of something much bigger.

Exposure comes in two forms:

1. You *see* something, and it activates a drive in you to want something. Your "wantingness" has increased due to exposure.
2. You *experience* something, and it activates a drive in you to want to repeat the experience.

Winning that first championship activated my drive for that feeling again. Speaking on that stage at 10X activated my hunger to be in front of more people. Making my first million in revenue in my company motivated me to do $10 million. Flying private for the first time—cruising at 30,000 feet and going at 500 miles per hour—opened my eyes to speed and convenience. Purchasing our home in Watercolor, Florida, taught me how to marry creativity with inspiration.

When Elon Musk was asked why he did what he did, he said he "read comic books as a child" and there was always a superhero trying to save the world. When Bill Clinton was 16, he met John F. Kennedy and was inspired to become president of the United States. When I was 25, I met Dr. Stephen Covey and was inspired to become an international thought leader. Exposure to someone or something will activate your drive.

Actually, for me it all began when I got a simple phone call from a mentor, asking me to help him coach. It was at this time that I started my coaching journey in junior pro basketball and fell in love with helping others drive their potential. I fell in love with the strategy, competition, and even embarrassment of losing, which drove me to activate and reactivate my drive.

This was also the time when a local dentist who had a love for theater and arts began mentoring me on speaking and communication. He chose me to be his mentee for one year, and I said yes. Every night after basketball practice, I would go to his house, and he would help me write, learn the art of speaking, and connect with people. This opened my eyes to skills and talents I had no idea I had and helped me refine those skills and talents I could put to use in life.

Thanks to this training and some success in a national honor society, I was lucky enough to go to the Broyhill Leadership Academy in North Carolina, where I was exposed to top thought leadership. I was scared to death: I had never been on a plane, away from home, or around other kids I didn't know. Going to North Carolina for one week to learn about leadership training and philosophy piqued my leadership and coaching interests and would eventually lead me to a life of leading other people toward their potential.

Many years ago, I wrote a book called *Small Towns and Big Dreams* because I wanted to share my story. I wanted to tell people what I just told you—about how I grew up in a small town where I learned my incredible values, and through exposure to bigger thinkers and expansive mindsets, I began to develop big dreams. Looking back on the cycle, I could codify it like this:

1. I had great coaches throughout my early life who instilled a discipline and grit in me that would be necessary to develop the persistence and intensity of the Prey Drive.

2. I had a mentor at 15 who taught me public speaking and writing skills (two of the most valuable skills a person could learn).

3. I went to a leadership camp at 15 that exposed me to bigger thinking and advanced leadership theory. (This was the Broyhill Leadership Academy and the inspiration for our Success Schools.)

4. I began studying under great leaders and coaches and observing their philosophies.

5. I began going to conferences and being exposed to people who had big dreams and were achieving bigger things than I was.

Each of these exposed and expanded me in ways I could not have imagined. Looking back now at 45, I can see clearly how all these important elements activated my Prey Drive. My goal now with our kids is to expose them to people who can expand their mind, keep their dreams activated, and give them the tools and confidence to win at the highest levels.

If it had not been for that *one coach* who called me to be his assistant coach and move to a bigger city and that *one coach* who would introduce me to that *one book* called *The 7 Habits of Highly Effective People*, I would have repeated the pattern of so many people who remain stuck in smallness.

It just takes *one*, so expose your kids to the world. Expose your employees to training and development. Expose yourself to the best. This can activate your Prey Drive because your mind has seen something that can trigger a bigger future. You have been turned on to something.

Don't allow yourself to fall complacent into believing that where you are is as big as you will ever get. Train your mind to be *open* to new people, new experiences, and better ways of operating.

EXPOSURE IS YOUR PRIMARY ACTIVATOR IF:

1. You are ultra-inspired when you are around others who think bigger, and this inspiration turns into action.
2. You love seeing new places or having your imagination expanded, and you convert these feelings of excitement into a new creation for you. Connecting with the energy of a new place or seeing something for the first time activates the imagination. It can open your mind to possibilities that you didn't know existed before.
3. You routinely place yourself around others who are doing much bigger numbers or outputs than you, and this excites and awakens something inside you that allows you to play at a bigger level.
4. You love the art of learning and applying that learning, and you constantly place yourself in the room where you can learn and apply, learn and apply. This could indicate that exposure is the primary activator of your Prey Drive.

WHO ARE YOU
ACTUALLY ACTIVATING?

In his book *Learned Optimism*, psychologist Martin Seligman noted that there are two types of people in the world: defensive pessimists (briefly mentioned earlier in the chapter) and strategic optimists.

A strategic optimist tends to show up and allow things to happen and generally believes everything will work out. On the other hand, a defensive pessimist mentally rehearses so that things don't go wrong. Both can have their Prey Drive activated; yet it may come from different activators.

Coach Nick Saban is said to be a defensive pessimist. He mentally rehearses everything that could go wrong so he can properly prepare for those scenarios. His desire to not be embarrassed activates the Prey Drive in him to work and rework at a higher pace. The embarrassment angle helps him be the best at what he does.

Is he successful? You bet! Saban clearly has the activation, the persistence, and the intensity that are needed to run high-level organizations, navigate the daily adversity and competition, and perform over and over again against intense competition.

WHAT WE LEARNED AND WHAT'S NEXT

In this chapter we focused on the five activators more deeply and how they relate to you personally, helping you move closer to your deepest potential, to clearly see what activates you, and to understand where you need to be pushed more. You've learned how to uncover the conditions that you have set for yourself and determine whether they are optimal or suboptimal when it comes to activating your Prey Drive.

As I look back over this chapter, it's clear to me that my drive is highest when:

I feel rejected or not good enough.

Someone doubts me and my skills.

I fear losing everything I've built.

There is a competition.

There could be an embarrassment if I don't perform well.

I am near people doing big things.

Now it's your turn to look back over the chapter. Once you have an awareness of what activates your Prey Drive and learn how to "call" on those activators, you will be unstoppable.

In the next chapter, we turn our attention to making your drive a daily habit.

How much Prey Drive do you actually have? Take the Prey Drive test to find out or share with your team to see how much they have.

CHAPTER 5

Going All In

How to Make Your Drive a Daily Habit

We are what we repeatedly do.
Excellence, then, is not an act, but a habit.

—WILL DURANT

"Today doesn't care what you did yesterday." This is a sentiment—a way of life—shared by all the top performers I've met, known, and coached. Activating your Prey Drive once is not a permanent flip of the switch. Without constant attention, the switch glitches, flickering on and off, which is why I teach managers and leaders of companies that above all else they need to activate and reactivate their drive every single day. This is the number one role of every leader. Beyond teaching skill. Beyond improving confidence. Beyond product knowledge. This is number one. Why? Because leaders can't engage their teams and help them flip their own switches if they themselves are dormant.

Unfortunately, many have not had training in activating a person's Prey Drive, leaving them frustrated and exhausted, constantly wondering why they can't keep themselves or their troops motivated. As a leader, your objective is not to activate the Prey Drive in your people, but rather to teach them how to activate it in themselves.

Many times there are long periods when I am out of the office and on the road. Because of this, it's essential that my team members (people who [I hope] already come with a big Prey Drive) know how to activate their own drive, even when I'm not there.

Making drive activation a habit can seem like a lofty endeavor. Any habit formation might feel that way. It requires discipline, commitment, and consistency, among other things, which is why there is an entire chapter in this book dedicated to strategies and tools to make this habit a reality on a day-to-day basis. Every day is a blank slate that requires certain practices in order to utilize your primary and secondary prey activators so that no opportunity goes uncapitalized. This chapter will help you make that happen.

THE PREY DRIVE *IS* YOUR DAY

The Prey Drive is not a bonus on top of your day, like a cherry on top of a sundae. It *is* your day. This is why I say so many times that nothing happens until the Prey Drive is activated. The ability to activate your Prey Drive all day, every day, instead of keeping it reserved for "certain moments," will make you a standout performer and an effective leader. The way I see it, going all in with the Prey Drive is what separates the pros from the amateurs. When it comes to gaining a competitive advantage, it's not IQ scores, physical quotient and skill, or past accomplishments. It's your ability to get up every single day and pursue something with an intensity and consistency and lock into the defining ambition while eliminating distraction and loss of focus. Consistency is defined by the *Oxford English Dictionary* as "the achievement of a level of performance that does not vary greatly in quality over time." And I believe it's one of the greatest missing structures in the world today. It's also one of the top topics people ask me to coach them on. The ability to do and do something again, especially when your thoughts and feelings might tell you otherwise, will put you in the top 5 percent of performers. The other 95 percent of the competitors simply wake up, go through the motions, and are not interested in peak performance.

Prey Drive and peak performance are two concepts uniquely tied together. Peak performance is the flow state that people enter when they are actualizing their potential. It's a flow and rhythm where time loses all meaning and you are lost in the moment. In their book *The Arc of Ambition*, James Champy and Nitin Nohria looked at how Thomas Jefferson pursued an opportunity and more important how he moved away from his comfort zone to pursue the opportunity. They wrote, "In 1803 Thomas Jefferson was president of a small republic with no power, scant cash, and fewer prospects—all of which pleased him. He dreaded bigness. A land of small farms, modest taxes, and minimal government was his idea of a perfect state. Even so, Jefferson was a man of boundless imagination and intelligence. Faced with an unexpected opportunity to vastly enlarge his country, he seized it."[1]

Notice the passage doesn't say Jefferson "thought about it," "asked someone else whether he should pursue it," "slept on it," or considered if "the timing was right." He *seized* it. Remember, the Prey Drive is an "instinct" to see something and pursue it even if it feels hard or the timing may not be right. Think back to an opportunity, a meeting, or a time when you could have changed your life but you chose instead to give in to your feelings of discomfort and didn't take action. We act our way into feeling. The next time you have a chance to enlarge your influence, whether that's through an opportunity or a relationship, I want this book to serve as a catalyst and reminder to you to do it.

THE CYCLE OF DRIVE

So how do we take the dimmer switch off your drive and create a daily Prey Drive habit that instinctually leads you to seize your opportunities? We consistently move through three important phases on a daily basis: activation, persistence, and intensity. Remember, the Prey Drive must be activated by something, likely one of the five activators we discussed in the last chapter. This activation is merely turning the key in the ignition of a sports car. Without the persistence of a skilled driver to go the distance, along with the intensity of the carefully engineered mechanics that make the car perform under hostile conditions, the engine is just idle under a hood.

———

In 2008, I was fresh off retiring from my role as a high school basketball coach and eager to begin my new career. This was an intense time: it was in the middle of a recession, and people were looking for solutions to a stagnant economy. Just at this time, a local real estate broker who had followed my sports coaching career hired me to be his team's coach. Old paradigms of real estate were being busted up, and the broker told me over lunch that he wanted to bring me in to stir the energy of the group.

What I found were people who were stuck in their old ways, internal politics at play, and people who needed to go. I went in each month and worked to activate the Prey Drive in the group. I had moderate success with some people, but others preferred to stay stuck and broke during this period and didn't get the most out of me as their coach.

One gentleman, named Tommy Davidson, stared at me intently during each session. Nicknamed "Good Time Tommy" for his antics, mindset, and partying nature, he was stuck doing 35 deals per year for over seven years with little or no professional Prey Drive to speak of. He never took a note, and many days I left feeling like he and the rest of the group were not making any progress and that they didn't have the persistence and intensity it takes to win. But eventually Tommy started understanding it.

Through exposure (his activator of the Prey Drive), he cultivated a hunger, not only to be better in his market, but to also use his past embarrassments of how other people treated him and make the ascension from number 43 in the market to number 1. Changing people's perceptions of him and internalizing a drive and work ethic day in and day out was going to be a big mountain for him to climb, but the sessions were definitely working.

Tommy signed up for our monthly coaching program called Monster Producer and dove headfirst into doing the work and becoming a "person of interest," which is a strategy of becoming known through our coaching. His Prey Drive for learning and pursuing came alive. Over the next seven years he would use two important phases of the Prey Drive (persistence and intensity) to climb from number 43 to number 1 and go from 35 transactions per year to over 300 transactions per year.

If we were dissecting what happened, I would boil it down to three steps, which can be replicated:

STEP 1. His Prey Drive was activated through exposure and embarrassment.

STEP 2. He cultivated the persistence of staying in the program for long cycles of time to reach mastery so he could become a teacher of the content to his team of real estate agents (now over 25 strong). This mastery would be important to scaling.

STEP 3. He used an intensity toward a clear B target, which was driven by his competitiveness and toughness to move toward being number 1 in one of the fastest-growing cities in the United States. Remember, he would be moving from number 43 to number 1.

When I asked him why the coaching worked for him and why he has stayed committed for so long while others start and quit, he said:

What you have really done for me is turn me into a coach of other people. I have mastered your content and have a depth of understanding of your systems and have used them to scale up. People can't do that in one year or even two years because they don't have an intimacy with the content. You have to live it. You have to dissect it. You have to internalize it before you can teach it to others with authority and help them get results. Then you have to manage to it to see that it gets done the right way. Too many start but quit way too early, and although they have an awareness of something, they do not have a deep awareness and mastery of it.

This is why the Prey Drive has three phases. Those people who just activate the drive may not have the persistence and intensity to see a thing through. Part of this has to do with their personality profiles (quick starts on the Kolbe Index), or these people may be lacking the strength to see something all the way through to its conclusion (StrengthsFinder test).

If you start with an awareness that eventually flickers out, you need to step back and ask yourself two questions: Why does your Prey Drive flicker out, and can you cultivate the muscles you need to see it through to its conclusion? I believe activating the Prey Drive is the easiest of the three. Seeing a bigger future when you are inspired is the easy part. Having the persistence and intensity to see that vision through to its manifestation is much harder, which is why so many never do it.

To begin this process you must cultivate an awareness of what you are actually good at. There are a number of tools to help figure this out, but many times I have people take the StrengthsFinder test. This kicks out your top five strengths. A quick look will show you exactly what you are strong at. Once you have an awareness of this, you can play to your strengths. I learned this the hard way in my own company by consistently trying to take on tasks I was weak in or hiring people and placing them in positions they couldn't be successful in and then trying to figure out why. The why was simple; they were not talented in these areas.

Once you have an awareness that persistence and intensity may not be in your wheelhouse, you have to make some hard decisions. Do I get better, or can I outsource this to someone who is skilled in it? Here's the problem: You can't outsource your own ambitions. Many times in life you will have to buckle down, embrace the suck, and see it through whether it's a strength or not. I'm a quick start by nature, which means I have more ideas than I can get to. The problem is that many of those ideas will generate millions of dollars, so I don't want to scale back my ideas. I just want to narrow down to the best ideas that I love doing, that solve big problems, and that produce great returns.

If you have a personal goal and ambition and your Prey Drive is activated, you simply can't say, "Well I'm good at coming up with the ideas and lousy at persisting toward the idea." At some point you have to do the work and persist with a key intensity and time compression to get it done.

Outline right here where you fail to follow through:

1. Activation of the drive:

   _____

2. Persistence of the drive:

   _____

3. Intensity of the drive:

   _____

A DEEPER LOOK AT PERSISTENCE

Persistence is defined as "firm or obstinate continuance in a course of action in spite of difficulty or opposition" (*Oxford English Dictionary*). In essence, persistence is the ability to "keep coming." Think of things in your own life right now where you continually say you are going to do something but then never follow through, creating a vicious cycle and ultimately causing the erosion of your confidence. Persistence is working the muscle until it becomes "muscle memory." But people struggle with this because it's not easy.

In one of my favorite books, *Long Obedience in the Same Direction,* author Eugene Peterson talks about the need to build repetition into your being when you are learning something, so that it becomes automatic and habitual. You don't question what you are doing. You just repeat.

Repetition harkens back to Anders Ericsson's 10,000-hour study, which was made famous in Malcolm Gladwell's book *Outliers.* In this study, Ericsson found that those who master their craft had logged more than 10,000 hours of practice while receiving evaluation, correction, and feedback from a coach or expert. Over the course of one's life, 10,000 hours equates to 1.14 years, and sticking with a practice to mastery for that long requires persistence. It's important to call out the fact that it wasn't just 10,000 hours of practice that made the difference; it was 10,000 hours of practice *with evaluation, coaching, feedback, and correction.*

The study went further to explain that the people learning must also receive explicit instructions about the best method to use for their training. This implies that the coach delivering this feedback is skilled at doing what the learners are trying to do.

This process of mastery is not for the faint of heart, but rather for those who really want to separate themselves, level up their performance, and become pros themselves. It comes down to cultivating daily habits that become part of who we are and refining the habits. Some of these habits include:

- Focusing on new money in the business every day by prospecting and presenting new ideas to people

- Blocking off concentrated periods of time to do nothing but focus on new money or engagement with current clients
- Following up 7 to 15 touches when people have indicated interest in your product or service
- Routinely staying in a flow and frequency with those in your ecosystem, keeping them top of mind
- Touching and tagging people with value to build new associations that can lead to new monetization by finding problems and offering compelling solutions

Persistence in the Workplace

Persistence is tricky because it requires people to sacrifice what they want *right now* in order to achieve what they want *later*. With persistence, the passion for the goal must be present, and there must be a consistency that you cultivate that takes an action and converts it to a habit. So when I see people not reaching what they say their goals are, it indicates to me that their passion to sacrifice in a way that supports persistence is absent.

Examples of this include people who want the six-pack abs without the sugarless diet, salespeople who want accolades at the next conference without learning or honing their selling skills, and entrepreneurs who want a business that's one step above but don't want to work on weekends.

However, when I see people persisting by following what they should be doing—by eating foods with no sugar, by taking sales courses or seeking mentorship, or by working round the clock at their business—that sacrifice to support persistence is clear. They live and breathe the message: "I am interested in mastery. I will put the work in. I will get the right coaching. I will take the feedback. I am interested in my deepest human potential. I will seek out the masters to teach me. This is my passion."

In the workplace, persistence looks very much the same as it does outside the workplace:

- Showing up early and staying until the job is done, not clocking out at a predetermined time
- Prospecting every day for 2½ hours minimum for nothing but new business
- Going 7 to 15 touches in the follow-up when a person is interested in doing business with you

Keep persisting toward results, not excuses, and you will "work the muscle" to move from A to B and do whatever it takes to take the vision of what you want your life to be like and turn it into a reality.

THE ROLE THAT INTENSITY PLAYS

Close your eyes and think about the people you know, admire, or have read about that seem to have figured out how to do everything and more, in almost all aspects of their life. We all know these "Energizer bunny" types, who have made the journey their life, and not the destination. Did you ever wonder . . .

- How do they go that hard every single day?
- How do they find the motivation to keep going after 30 years?
- How do they handle the disappointment they face when people let them down?
- How do they do it over and over again?
- How do they pivot failure?

- How do they get their Prey Drive back once they've lost it or it has gone dormant?

The answer is intensity.

The top echelon of people in any domain have mastered intensity and put in the work to consistently ensure it's nurtured and incorporated in every pursuit.

Being *intense*, defined by the *Oxford English Dictionary* as "of extreme force, degree, or strength," is the final piece of the Prey Drive. Think of intensity as the power or ferocity of attack.

Big-time people have a vision and use intensity to:

- Work unceasingly with force and power to achieve that vision.
- Eliminate low-value activities and focus on bringing an idea to its logical conclusion.
- Avoid messing around with our most precious commodity—time.
- Be on offense, not defense.
- Take risks other people can't understand.
- Create uncommon energy about them that others can't keep up with.
- Avoid burnout; they merely refuel.

Remember the people we visualized who seem to be at it at all hours of the day, every day? Let's look at the questions these people are asked most frequently so we can see that what they accomplish is a habit of drive.

1. **HOW DO YOU GO THAT HARD EVERY SINGLE DAY?**
   Top performers believe success and confidence come from repetition, role play, and performance. They believe in "chopping wood and carrying water," and

that it all goes to zero at midnight, meaning they disallow complacency to set in as they have only enough food for the day.

I learned from my days as a basketball coach something that would help me tremendously when I started my own business: I don't allow myself to grow complacent. I have a deep desire to be the best, and the best requires lots of reps. When you learn to fight through the fatigue that comes with those reps, fighting through fatigue becomes a habit and part of your normality.

2. **HOW DO YOU FIND THE MOTIVATION TO KEEP GOING AFTER SO MANY YEARS?** Many get bored when they don't have something new to pursue. Nobody said it would be fun all the time, or consistently entertaining, or always exciting. In today's world, many want instant gratification and immediate results without doing the work. They don't want to make the sacrifices it actually takes to achieve a better life. Many don't realize how much time they will have to spend on the road away from family or have to stay in hotel rooms by themselves; nor do they realize how much preparation it takes to be great, which is a daily discipline. Like great athletes, true professionals do the deep work it takes to be great, but first they have the proper expectation of how hard that work is going to be.

For me personally, there are a few ways I seek to reactivate my drive, including finding new problems to tackle, new goals to pursue, and new targets that excite me, typically ones that are big and scary. My goal is to never stagnate with the same goals, yet still have an intense curiosity that prompts me to study bigger people, expand my mindset, and get excited about some future target. For many, it's not the end result of capturing their targets that motivates them, but rather it's in the doing—the intense pursuit of those targets.

If you are like me, you may be most motivated when in pursuit of something big and exciting, and many times that may scare you. If I feel stagnant or believe that I'm not making progress toward a big goal, I become restless. Take an area of your life that you have a deep curiosity about and pursue it. Study something new; identify an area that needs improvement; go study under someone who is a master at a craft. This will excite you again and get you out of a bored or complacent state.

3. **HOW DO YOU HANDLE DISAPPOINTMENT?** There is a lot of disappointment in the coaching business. It's a game you really can't win no matter how good you are to people or how much money you help them make. No matter how good they feel when you leave, some will turn on you, be disgustingly mean to you, and publicly slander you. Many go to a coach and expect the coach to "change them" or "save them," when they are not really willing to do the work. When you understand human nature—and that is, we start with good intentions, we fail to follow through, and then we experience guilt—you then understand that it's not personal, and you don't take it personally.

I've done all kinds of things to help people, only to do one thing they didn't like and get the nastiest messages you could ever imagine. At first it's heartbreaking, but then if you allow it to become a distraction, you are only participating in the drama. All of that has happened to me both as a basketball coach and as a business coach. You have to make up your mind that when you do big things in the world, there will be opposition. There will be people who by their own nature can't allow you to win. Miserable with their own tiny lives and a small or nonexistent Prey Drive, they actually take joy in trying to tear you down, but they can't. This frustrates them. Allow it to fuel you. My strategy on disappointment is simple. If you are helping a small number of people and a few let you down, it's disappointing. If you are helping hundreds of thousands of people and a few bozos let you down, it doesn't even phase you. The solution is to help more people so you don't even notice.

4. **HOW DO YOU DO IT OVER AND OVER AGAIN?**
   Remember that 10,000-hour rule that says that you need 10,000 hours of practice and requires deep intense work in concentrated areas with little or no distraction? My goal is to live by this and know that mastery comes through deep work and many times lots of monotony. This work may seem boring and disinteresting, but it is through the continual repetition that one builds a deep intimacy with something and converts that to mastery. I believe there is a direct correlation between how strong a person's skills are and how much money that person creates.

   It's important to remember that you don't master something by starting and stopping. There must be a consistency, and you must "do the work." I believe in *mastery*, and I believe those who are truly the best will master something. It's working as a craftsperson building something beautiful that reactivates your Prey Drive and recharges your enthusiasm repeatedly. It's the thrill of working and trying something new and exciting or coming at something old in a new way. The masters spend a portion of their time under a master (me under Dr. Stephen Covey for 8 years). They then practice what they see the master do (me coaching for 12 years, followed by teaching the concepts and refining the primary skill). They then become a master (me today trying every day to activate that Prey Drive to do something bigger). If you are serious about mastery, you must learn that success can become boring. It can lose its meaning if you are not careful and you let it. This is why you have to learn to measure progress and not perfection. You get up and kick everybody's butt and then do it all over again the next day. I'm motivated by the hunt, the exposure to something bigger, and the massive impact I can make in the world.

5. **WHERE DOES YOUR INTENSITY COME FROM?** Over the years, I've learned that I'm driven, focused, and dominant (and sometimes difficult to deal with). I'm angry and frustrated that I don't get where I want to be fast enough, and this makes me intense.

Some are wired to be intense, and some are not, but there can also be a quiet intensity about you toward a target even if this is not your personality style. Remember, intensity is a focus with an energy toward a target. The goal here is to move with purpose and intention and to tie high-value activity to your schedule daily to achieve something you think is meaningful to you.

6. **HOW DO YOU GET YOUR PREY DRIVE BACK IF YOU HAVE LOST IT OR IT HAS GONE DORMANT?** First, it's important to understand that if your Prey Drive has been deactivated, it's likely because you aren't making progress toward a target. You can reactivate your drive in a number of ways, including changing environments, increasing exposure to mentors and models, and creating lots of movement and circulation around key relationships that could produce new opportunities.

In many cases people's best ideas are stimulated when they aren't under pressure to perform and they are in a relaxed setting where their mind can go out to play. Intensity can quickly be reignited by being in the presence of people doing significant things or sticking around people and places that give you energy (think back to the environment we talked about in Chapter 4).

If you've lost your Prey Drive, I suggest moving locations such as working somewhere new to gain new energy, going where there is new opportunity or new money, or getting around people who are operating at higher frequencies and playing in bigger arenas. This change of locations can change your energy. Just yesterday I started my day with coaching Zooms at 7:30 a.m. until noon from my home office. I stopped, ate lunch, and then went for a bike ride of 20 minutes and listened to something motivational. This was exactly what I needed to break up my day, reactivate my Prey Drive, and go into the second part of the day with a fresh perspective and a hungry drive. I also suggest making sure you are taking care of you, specifically your body (physical), mind (mental), heart (passion), and spirit (confidence).

Start the Day with the Three Phases

Activation, persistence, and intensity require the right conditions, and those conditions are set by you, the very minute you wake up. Begin the day early enough to do the small things that signal our brains that we are in charge, confident, capable, and connected to our goals and to those around us.

So many of the most successful people in the world carve out this time to think, meditate, and exercise. Successful people tap into their Prey Drive each day before they execute. Do you think Michael Jordan showed up 15 minutes before work?

If you want to make the most of each day, you will need large amounts of "attractive energy"—which I think of as the energy that pulls other people toward you. In the business jungle either you can spend all your time chasing leads, trying to convince people to do business with you, and trying to sell them, or you can work on becoming attractive to the market by creating incredible concepts that solve key problems in the world that others would move toward.

Hopping out of bed in a mad dash to get ready for work, gulping down coffee, and not fueling your body with nutrients that will support your energy is not going to give you that attractive energy. In fact, people who are successful and have this attractive energy know that a morning ritual and a nutrition plan are at least as important as networking, taking courses, or burning the midnight oil, if not more important.

Here are some ideas to get your started, well before the rest of your competitors have pressed "brew" on their Keurig:

- **"TUNE" IN.** I wake up to music each day because it changes my state of mind. I currently listen to two songs: "It's a Great Day to Be Alive" and "I'm Going to Be Somebody Someday," both by Travis Tritt. These songs connect to my core values of gratitude and ambition, which inspires my *heart*. It's hard to start off the day the wrong way when you start in gratitude.
- **FEED YOUR SPIRIT.** I listen to a 20-minute sermon, because I'm a person of deep faith. I typically listen to Pastor Jimmy Evans, who founded Marriage Today, which is a marriage ministry that helps people build healthy marriages. He tackles lots of subjects and breaks the Bible down into simple terms that I appreciate. He also tackles fear, insecurity, doubt, and worry. This feeds my *spirit*. Remember, our goal is to tackle all four parts of our nature: body, mind, heart, and spirit.

  Other ways to feed your spirit could be to listen to positive podcasts, use daily affirmations, practice a form of meditation, or make space for quiet time to reflect and think about the impact you are supposed to be having on the world today.
- **SPEND TIME WITH THOSE YOU LOVE (INCLUDING PETS).** I spend time with my wife and kids, typically over breakfast, connecting with them and talking about the goals of the day. This also feeds my *heart* and is good for my soul. With a hectic schedule, having

meaningful moments and creating a baseline for my family is vital to the activation of my Prey Drive. A baseline is a commitment to start at a certain point and get that time in daily before moving to other things or overextending yourself in areas and not feeding the most important relationships in your life.

- **EXERCISE.** I exercise for 40 minutes each morning and like to mix it up. Currently I enjoy boxing at a place called RockBox Fitness. This feeds my creativity (my *mind*) and gives my *body* a workout. I do this at 5 a.m., which really makes me enforce a bedtime ritual, ensuring I get enough sleep to be up by 4:20 a.m. You really don't have to go hard core; the goal is to get your body moving and your blood pumping to your heart and brain. Running up and down your stairs, walking around the block, and even stretching will make a huge difference in how you feel as you head out into the world.

  Ending a day feeling exhausted and being in the battle of running a small business can be tough. This is why I like to exercise in the mornings. It sets the tone for the day, gets my endorphins working, and opens my mind to possibility. There's just something about tackling this first thing in the morning that activates my Prey Drive and sets me in a mindset of playing offense versus defense.

- **ENRICH YOUR MIND.** I finish my morning routine by listening to 10 to 20 minutes of content about business while I get ready for my day. This feeds my *mind*, gets me ready to go into battle, and sets the tone for me to (once again) play offense versus defense, which gets me in a mindset of creation.

- **PUSH THROUGH RESISTANCE.** Most mornings I create
  and post a 10-minute coaching video on Facebook.
  I really don't always *feel* like doing this, but when I
  make my goals for the daily public, it adds a layer of
  accountability to my life.

  Resistance or inertia like this is normal. You'll
  likely experience some friction when you begin a new
  habit or task, but this is something you have to learn
  how to deal with if you want to leave your amateur
  desires behind and go pro. Very few people wake up
  and want to go to the gym, shoot a video, make an
  outbound call, or follow up on a deal. The brain loves
  the path of least resistance, but the greats overcome this
  inertia and learn the process of taking an action that
  could produce a result.

- **INITIATE THE PREY DRIVE IN OTHERS.** Finally to wrap
  up my morning, I meet with my team at 8:45 a.m.
  CST. This excites me. I love pouring ideas into others
  who are hungry to improve themselves. For all the
  leaders who are reading this, never underestimate the
  need to activate and reactivate that drive every single
  morning for yourself and those on your team. Many
  need a stimulus to put them into a forward posture
  toward their goals—and that can be anything from
  an affirmation, a word of encouragement, or some
  direction that activates their drive to move and take
  action. Remember, your team is made up of people,
  and those people most likely struggle with inertia
  themselves. They may come into the office beat up
  emotionally or overwhelmed with life. Something or
  someone has to initiate their Prey Drive and help them

start up their engine to attack the day. Be that someone for them.

DOING DEEP WORK: THE ESSENCE OF DAILY HABITS

The key to creating morning rituals is to incorporate elements that nurture the four components of our nature: body, mind, heart, and spirit. Different behaviors and practices are more suitable for one component than another. So when experimenting with your morning ritual, think of feeding each part of your nature and activating your Prey Drive in these ways:

1. Do intense exercise with a coach in an environment that pushes you to play at a high level and fight through mental constraints or in an environment that activates your drive for your *body*.
2. Listen to podcasts or read today's business news in your favorite trade journal to activate your *mind*.
3. Take time with your family and/or friends and pets, connecting your *heart* to your greater purpose or to something that feeds your *heart*.
4. Meditate, read a poem, practice a gratitude exercise, or read a Bible passage that feeds your *spirit*.

Millions of people fail to have a morning routine and barely make it through their days. They start poorly and head in the wrong direction from the beginning. Think of it like a game. We start. We accelerate. We finish. We rest and rejuvenate. The greats see themselves as high-performance people of interest. They are persons of advancement and give off the *impression of increase,* which is a feeling of improvement and advancement that people can only give off when they are advancing themselves This feeling of increase comes from their knowledge, skills, desire, and contagious confidence. It's an energy that people give off that has to do with how they see themselves. But you can't give off an energy that you don't possess. This is why the Prey Drive is so critical to this equation. Until your Prey Drive is activated, nothing happens. There is no fire. There is no energy. There is nothing but static behavior, and you will never experience a breakthrough with this mindset or the action items.

In his book *Deep Work,* Cal Newport talks about Carl Jung, the famous psychologist who built a retreat on the shore of Lake Zurich in the village of Bollingen. Jung picked a spot and built a two-story round house that came to be called the Tower. After a trip to India, where he observed the practice of meditation, he expanded the complex and added a private office. Up at 7 a.m. daily, he would eat a big breakfast and spend two hours of uninterrupted time in his private office. The afternoons consisted of meditations or long walks. Jung would say, "The feeling of repose and renewal that I had in the Tower was intense from the start." This routine allowed Jung to go deeper into his thought processes and created an environment for his Prey Drive to be activated daily so he could "do the important work" he was supposed to be doing in the world, and he created a place to do that without distractions.

This example reminds me of the importance of your morning routine to activate and reactivate your drive to prepare for that day's performance so you can do the deep work needed for you to move ahead in the world. You need to be doing "deep work," not "shallow work." If you don't take yourself seriously enough, you will stay up too late, sleep in too much, and see today just like you did yesterday.

WHAT WE LEARNED AND WHAT'S NEXT

The lessons here are simple:

Remember that your Prey Drive is supported by your habits and daily wins.

Do like the greats do. Go into battle every single day. Wake up daily, and work to activate and reactivate that drive so you can do the important work you are supposed to be doing.

And always consider what feeds your soul, what accelerates your heart, and what makes you think.

In the next chapter we focus on how to create value in the world, and you will learn to be a contender.

 Watch this video as Coach Burt breaks down his morning Prey Drive activators to get in a state to perform.

CHAPTER 6

Creating Value in the World

Becoming a Contender

Do the best you can until you know better.
Then when you know better, do better.
—MAYA ANGELOU

For most of us, action equals success in our careers, business ventures, side hustles, and innovations. Action means being valuable to the world and creating value in it. When activating the Prey Drive, there is usually a crossroads that separates those who have staying power and those who fizzle out like a shooting star. Those who pretend to have a Prey Drive and those who contend by activating theirs. Ultimately the Prey Drive should be converted to opportunity and monetization; otherwise it's just a constant pursuit of something that never materializes. How many talented people do you know that struggle to convert the Prey Drive into money or opportunity? As a coach, I see thousands daily that get up and go to work and are actually busy; yet they can't seem to convert that work into a better life, and certainly can't convert it into money, which helps build a better life.

I have worked with many people over the course of my lifetime who showed flashes of brilliance and flashes of the Prey Drive, but many times could not take an idea and see it through to its logical conclusion (a big topic I talk about daily with my team). These people didn't have a fully activated Prey Drive, and most important, they lacked the consistency needed to activate it every day. They were victims of their moods or feelings, which indicated to me that they had not graduated to the majors. Those destined to play in the minor leagues remain amateurs. Amateurs have an amateur impact, ultimately make amateur money, and typically deeply overvalue their skill sets living in some false reality that overexaggerates their real value in achieving the end result. Instead of letting their work do the talking, their mouth does, and it rarely ends in any kind of meaningful result.

I once worked with a real estate agent who advertised himself as "The Million Dollar Agent." He would buy two-page newspaper spreads talking up his expertise. A quick look at his actual results revealed that he was doing fewer than 10 deals per year and most likely earning less than $50,000. He was a pretender, not a contender. In our Instagram and TikTok world, pretenders are everywhere. You don't want to be one of these people.

It's quite easy to be able to tell the difference between contenders and pretenders and ascertain the level of their Prey Drive, and therefore the value they can have in the world of business. Just listen to the language of the pretender:

"It didn't work for them; therefore, it probably won't work for me."

- Pretenders lean on gossip, drama, and things that happened in the past, usually things they don't have firsthand knowledge of, rather than finding out for themselves They spend large amounts of time in low-value activity that is not fruitful.
- Contenders lean on their own experiences and spend their time in high-value activity, which is activity that leads them toward their B.

"What do you think about that game this past week?"

- Pretenders talk about events—their exploits on Friday night or the weekend, sports, the weather, or something they look forward to. They constantly think about things that help them escape the daily grind, and they put down the efforts of those who are more accomplished.
- Contenders are not in the stands; they are on the field. They are not spectators in life. They are actually in the arena making it happen, and if they haven't yet figured out how to be in the arena, you better believe they are working on it. They pursue relationships, partnerships, deals, and potential with an obsessive nature

"I didn't close the deal today. I don't think the buyers were qualified; I don't think they had the money."

- Pretenders always find a reason outside themselves why something didn't work or convert to a deal.
- Contenders self-reflect; talk ideas, tactics, and strategies; and look for recalibrations to make it work.

Where there is interest, there is a way, and contenders keep going until they find that opening.

"That's a great idea. We should do that going forward. I'll resolve the problems so we can make those ideas a part of our regular practice going forward."

- Pretenders talk a big game but rarely solve the problem.
- Contenders talk about and implement the execution of ideas, tactics, and strategies. They follow up and bring ideas to a close. They stay in the game until it's complete. They become incredibly valuable to an organization because they are action-oriented versus suggestion-oriented. They show real results and really move the needle toward the defining ambition.

———

Contenders *do*—they have that demonstrated capacity of *doing*. Pretenders talk, seldom follow through, and don't really know how to activate or reactivate their drive. This erodes their trust not only in themselves but in many others around them.

Let's take an even deeper look at the differences between contenders and pretenders.

CONTENDERS VERSUS PRETENDERS

A contender is a person who is in the arena fighting. You typically can tell quickly that people are contenders by the results and progress they are making and the reputational capital they bring to the equation. They are doers and achievers.

A pretender is a person who is outside the arena, many times criticizing the one on the inside.

Contenders are motivated to take an idea and pursue it persistently and patiently. This can take a significant amount of time to test, retest, and get feedback so you can tweak an idea, find its sweet spot, and become a master for the future.

Contenders are less focused on image and put more energy toward mastery, meaning they want to be people of substance versus people of images. Robert Greene's work on mastery gives us a road map for the serious person:

- First, you study under a master, which is typically 4 to 7 years. This could be by emotionally identifying with the master and studying the work deeply, or you might serve an actual apprenticeship.
- Second, you practice what you see the master do, which is typically a 4-to-7-year process. This could be where you implement what you are observing from the master in your own setting, or you are physically working under the master observing and practicing.
- Finally, you become a master, and others seek to learn from you. In this case you have mastered the skills by internalizing them and showing a demonstrated capacity to execute on them. You are now becoming a leader to others through your skills and Prey Drive.

The activation of the Prey Drive and the persistence and intensity of the Prey Drive determine whether a person will do the work to truly become a person of interest that other people will follow. Until this cycle has been implemented, many are still pretenders who simply want to be contenders. Contenders start things and finish things. Amateurs start many things but never finish anything. This becomes an ongoing problem that plagues them their entire lives. Money problems and constant stress join forces to give them an overall feeling of overwhelm.

For example, it would be naïve for me to believe I could take a job in an industry I know nothing about and within the first six months be an expert in that industry. Unfortunately, though, this naïveté runs rampant today. Because of the low barriers to entry in many domains, there is now a plague of pretenders, specifically in my field of coaching and consulting. Don't be one of these people. Instead, get in the arena. Experience wins and losses. Activate and reactivate your Prey Drive over long cycles of time. Define and refine your skill set. And demonstrate your capacity that you have something very valuable to say that other people would find valuable enough to pay for.

Once you do all of that, you will have demonstrated a capacity to actually teach, coach, and lead other people. You will have lived what you preach and shown high levels of competency of doing it.

HOW TO USE YOUR "BECAUSE GOALS" TO GO FROM PRETENDER TO CONTENDER

So now that you understand the difference between a pretender and a contender, how do you become the latter?

You must have a desire to move from pretending to contending. You need to *want* to do something big in order to actually do something big. To make this happen, you must remove the low-value activities you currently spend your time participating in. These are activities you engage in that do not produce a fruit or a revenue. For instance, do you spend time talking about events, other people, or what happened or could happen? *Or* do you focus on specific activities that move you closer to your B? Every action you take should be moving you from A to B. Remember, A is your current location in life. B is your desired ideal outcome, and getting there requires you to be clear on your "Because Goals."

What are Because Goals? Because Goals are the big reasons you want to do something. You want to do a certain thing *because* you have a deep psychological and emotional reason to take an action versus sit on the sidelines. Here are some examples of Because Goals:

- You may have grown up with not very much or considered yourself poor. *Because* of this, you made a vow early in life to work hard and create surplus and abundance.
- You may not have had a parent present in your early life. *Because* of this, you may want to ensure you are not an absentee parent, but are fully present with your kids.
- You may have a desire to help a certain group of people *because* someone helped you during a rough transition in life.
- *Because* someone believed in you when you didn't believe in you, you may have a desire to mentor other people who are low on confidence and need additional guidance.

When coaching people to discover their Because Goals, I invite them to do some exercises. And now I'd like to invite you do to the same.

Write out your Because Goals. Take your time and write down the big reasons you are willing to do something even when you don't feel like doing whatever it is. Your Because Goals should prompt you to take action, because they are tied to an intrinsic motivator (and potentially one of your Prey Drive activators, too). When I look at my Because Goals, I can see that they are tied to some big reason why I want to take action, even when I don't feel like it. Here are some big examples:

- *Because* I stayed in cheap hotels for many years, I made up my mind I was going to generate enough money to stay in nicer hotels and suites for my emotional well-being.
- *Because* a good coach changed my life, I made up my mind I was going to go into the coaching profession to help others activate their potential.
- *Because* I believe that where there is no money, there is no mission, I made up my mind I was going to focus on revenue generation every single day with a key target to make the business go. Notice that the action begins because of the deep Because Goals and the intrinsic motivation that results by being clear on the Because Goals.

Revisit your A to B goals. Your A goal represents your current position in life, and your intention is to move toward your B goal—your desired position. Your B goal is most likely something you *want*, but you may lack the motivation to move toward B if you don't have strong enough Because Goals. If your B is not big enough or your Because Goals are not strong enough, you may stay in limbo between A and B. My Because Goals prompt me to take action even when my feelings tell me otherwise. Our goals serve as constant reminders that motivate us, which is why getting crystal clear on them is so important. Are you getting clear on your B?

If it helps you to see the Because Goals of others, here are several that prompt me to want to take action when I don't feel like it:

- Growing up, though I didn't want for anything, I didn't have a lot. *Because* of this, I want to experience the luxuries of life, and I am willing to make outbound calls, follow up, and push to hit sales goals to create income for a life I am proud of.
- I didn't have both parents fully involved early in my life. *Because* of this, I will prioritize spending time with my children.
- I do not want to be dependent on others or place my destiny in other people's hands. *Because* of this, I will find the way and the people needed to achieve my target.

There will be moments when you need motivation to stay on track. Your Because Goals will help you do exactly that.

THE PREY DRIVE AND THE CONFIDENCE CONNECTION

I define "confidence" as "the memory of success." True confidence comes from remembering what you are good at and are practiced in. Confidence is also possessing the knowledge that you can create what you see in your mind even when others don't think you can. This comes from repetition and ultimately becomes muscle memory—your ability to do something without thinking. Confidence is also an act of distributing your talents to the world and receiving positive feedback (think of the response of an audience to an artist). The positive feedback and positive results you get from the distribution of your talents to solve a problem for the world builds your confidence, and this encourages you to take the action again and get another positive result. The positive feedback actually reactivates the Prey Drive over and over again and ignites your fire for more. It's an ongoing, drive-activating cycle.

When you connect to your activator, you exude confidence. Because you tried and received positive feedback, you will have removed the considerations (internal thoughts) of fear, embarrassment, rejection, or anything else that would talk you out of achieving your goal.

To sum up, you apply your talent to a problem you enjoy solving, and you help another person by doing so. That person gives you positive feedback and activates your confidence to go for it with more people. This is ultimately how great businesses are started and monetized. It's a magical thing when you discover what problem you want to solve and are uniquely qualified to do so. The result is confidence—and becoming a true contender.

On the other hand, pretenders never get the real feedback because they never deliver on the promise. This only continues to erode their false confidence. Many live in what's called a "false positive," which is where you begin to believe you are really better than what you are.

As I mentioned earlier, specifically in the world of coaching, we're living in a world where people haven't worked their muscles enough. They haven't gotten in the arena and fought enough. They don't have that skill that truly solves a problem for another. They've inflated their numbers, their skill sets, their results, and even their looks with filters on social media. All their confidence comes from likes and shares on social media (which can be purchased). The pretenders *look like* they are good but really are not.

Pretenders hide behind fake profiles and numbers while contracting to places of comfort. Confident people expand and pursue their potential. Which are you going to be?

WHAT WE LEARNED AND WHAT'S NEXT

To go from a pretender (one who talks about doing) to a contender (one who is in the arena fighting to win), you need to have your Because Goals and an unshakable confidence in yourself.

The next chapter continues to highlight the importance of confidence as you learn how to create a sales system and close the deal.

 Are you a *contender* or a *pretender*? Take this test to find out and get Coach's seven ways to contend.

CHAPTER 7

Flipping the Switch on Selling

Creating a Sales System and Closing the Deal

Our greatest weakness lies in giving up.
The most certain way to succeed
is always to try just one more time.
—**THOMAS EDISON**

n the *Merriam Webster Dictionary*, one of the definitions of the word "close" is to "to bring or come to an end." And this can be anything, including an idea, partnership, or opportunity. In sales, the goal is to close a deal. This skill of closing is sorely missing in today's society. In a very distracted world, many leave open loops with no feedback or fail to bring opportunities or situations to a close.

To close anything in life, you're going to need two things: confidence and certainty. Selling and closing are all about confidence, which creates certainty and breeds more confidence. The cycle of presenting and recalibrating is vital to building, maintaining, and protecting your confidence and is restored every time you take an action.

In his book *Atomic Habits*, James Clear refers to a gentleman who gets up every morning and drives to the gym but stays for no more than five minutes. Most would laugh at this, knowing that going only for five minutes will not do anything for your body. Clear makes the argument that the mere fact of getting up every morning, putting on your gym clothes, driving to the gym, and going in, albeit it for five minutes, is actually building a habit. Many never even take this first step, so five minutes becomes better than nothing. And, in fact, the habit building alone is a huge gain. The moral of the story: each move you make builds the muscle a little bit stronger until it becomes strong enough to keep you going, even in the face of adversity or unwanted outcomes.

In the sales world many lack the confidence to even pick up the phone to make an outbound effort that will put them in a position to win. This fear plagues millions of people who have a desire to make more money but can't seem to create a sale. I know that life is a game of probability and that less than 16 percent of prospects will be open and inviting to your offer on the first try. This is why you need the confidence to make eighty calls, not just one. With every call, you get better and better. Knowing this, you need to keep trying over and over to gain the confidence to close the deal. And you also need to continually understand what products people need to solve their problems. This clarity will lead to the yes that closes the deal.

Confidence is vitally important to the salesperson who has gone three days without a sale and is thinking of giving up or giving in versus getting up (again) or digging in. Confidence is vitally important to the leader who has tried multiple initiatives to engage the team, and still nothing seems to work.

People facing a challenge when it comes to selling need their Prey Drive to be activated. Why? Because that's what gets you to persist in those down cycles of confidence. There are no wasted movements when it comes to building your confidence. Every move you make, every action you take, is a gain of knowledge and skill, not a loss, even if you don't get the results you hoped for.

THE PREY DRIVE AND SELLING

With confidence, clarity, and a well-honed Prey Drive, you hold the tools to convince others to enroll in your mission, buy your products, join your team, or use you and your talents. People are attracted to action, boldness, movement and circulation in the world, and confidence. An established Prey Drive keeps you from getting caught up in the emotions of selling and the inevitable noes that could erode your confidence. An established Prey Drive allows you to use the tough parts of selling as activators rather than disablers.

Now that we know all of this, let's tie your Prey Drive and your confidence to selling and monetizing your unique skills and talents, or what I like to call your *special*. Many times you are not selling a product or service. Instead you are offering a special set of skills and abilities that solves a problem for the consumer. You have a unique way of delivering a solution based on your past that allows for differentiation from your competition. The clearer you are in those unique skills you possess, the more confidence you are going to display when helping others. The distribution of your skills to solve a unique problem with the positive feedback from the market is going to activate and reactivate your Prey Drive.

To find your special skill set, you have to look into the past. Your past is where the raw materials lie that helped make you uniquely qualified to help others. In essence, you can help other people solve their problems because you used to be those other people. You had their problems and found a way to work through those problems, and you have most likely developed a unique process that will solve their problems. This process, based on what you have learned, combined with your unique skills and talents becomes incredibly valuable to others. In the end this is what you are really selling, and it's what gets you out of the commodity business and ultimately into the transformation business.

The best salespeople have a conviction about their product or service and many times have been transformed by it. This unique transformation and conviction will enable them to use their talents and unique skill sets to create concepts or products and services that solve unique problems in the world, or what I classify as recurring problems. These are problems that you might see over and over and over, and yet no one has solved them. This is a prime opportunity to use your skills to solve a problem and create monetization. Your solution must be packaged into something consumers can feel, touch, taste, or smell. In other words, it must be packaged into a form people can consume. And like other consumables, it must be marketed and promoted to people who have the time, money, and resources to pay for it. Dan Sullivan calls this "the fundamental relationship," which is the relationship between your skill and a person's problem. In the center of this transaction, there is monetization. Money changes hands when problems are solved. Therefore, selling is just locating a problem and offering a compelling solution to that problem.

Many times potential customers don't know how much you can help them until you show them. Showing them is the sales process. We don't "sell" or "pitch." We "offer" and "invite" people to go deeper with us so we can solve a problem for them with our talents or services. There is an art to selling and an art to making money, which is coming up with unique products and services that solve unique problems. My guess is, you've had an instinct about something that would help another person. That instinct is the Prey Drive. And actually capitalizing on that Prey Drive is seeing the idea through to its logical conclusion, meaning your product is monetized.

Here's what you do to monetize your product:

1. **FIND YOUR UNIQUE SKILL THAT WOULD SOLVE A PROBLEM.** You do this by looking into your past and doing the heavy lifting on what makes you unique.

2. **PACKAGE THAT SKILL INTO A WAY OTHERS CAN CONSUME THE SKILL.** Packaging a concept is taking your unique process and placing it into something that others can consume. I package my intellectual property into books, programs, audios, speaking engagements, one-day events, boot camps, strategic partnerships, and more.

3. **MARKET THAT SKILL TO THOSE WHO MIGHT NEED IT.** Marketing is the distribution of a message to people who have a problem.

4. **MONETIZE THAT SKILL BY USING IT TO SOLVE A KEY PROBLEM.** Money is exchanged when a problem is solved.

Which part of this cycle do you currently struggle with?

If money changes hands when problems are solved, you can wake up daily and solve small problems ("Blue Gills") or big problems ("Blue Marlins"). You can capitalize on the biggest opportunities available to you (Level 10 opportunities), or you can stay stuck chasing small opportunities that tie up your time and energy (Level 1 opportunities). You can help one person, or you can help millions of people. To sell, you have to utilize an outbound effort, which is the process of generating leads, working those leads, and bringing those leads to a close by offering your product or service to solve the prospect's problem. You have to initiate. You have to make contact. You have to get attention. You have to keep attention. You have to explain your value, elicit interest, follow up on that interest, and ultimately bring a deal to a close, which means to bring two things together and bring something to an end.

All of this takes three things:

1. **THE INSTINCT TO PURSUE.** To really go get it. This is the activation daily of the Prey Drive.

2. **THE CONFIDENCE TO ARTICULATE AND COMMUNICATE WITH STRANGERS.** This is the persistence of the Prey Drive to keep going when you hear no a lot. This is uncomfortable and places you in a position to feel rejected, which is why so many never do it.

3. **THE SKILL TO CLOSE SOMEONE AND EXCHANGE YOUR TALENT FOR THE PERSON'S MONEY.** This is the intensity it takes to close, to ask someone to make a decision, and to remove a consideration to go for

the close. This is the true conversion from interest to activation of the client.

I believe money doesn't buy you freedom. I believe skills buy you freedom. Selling your skills will generate money you can use to build the freedom you are looking for. Now we are drawing a correlation between your confidence, your drive, and your skills. Your income is in direct proportion to your knowledge, your skills, your desire, and your confidence. If you are not making the income you wish, it indicates to me you are either not very good (skill) or simply in the wrong vehicle. Some of you don't have a talent problem but instead may have a Prey Drive problem or a marketing problem.

It takes a special dose of the Prey Drive to ask another to take an action, and many will never develop this ability, therefore leaving them limited in their money-generating capacity forever. My hope is that this book will remove any considerations you might have about asking others for something. All they can do is tell you no. All they can do is say, "I'm not interested." None of this is life or death. If you have fear in any of these areas, ask yourself if the fear is in proportion to the outcome. If it's not, then you should remove the fear and allow the Prey Drive and instinct to lead you.

SELLING REQUIRES A SYSTEM

After coaching thousands of sales professionals and small business owners, I've found that 9 out of 10 people do not have a *system* to grow their business. It baffles me. The purpose of any business is to acquire a customer, and without a system, you aren't going to be able to do that.

To create your selling system, you must first understand why and how the Prey Drive is necessary. Your Prey Drive will lead you to be deeply engaged in your selling system and will in turn give you the confidence to:

- Initiate.
- Present an idea.
- Follow up.
- Overcome opposition.
- Bring something to a close.
- Deliver consistently on what you sold.
- Repeat the cycle of finding and locating problems in the marketplace over and over again.
- Grow from a person of interest into a person of expansion.

Once you understand the importance that the Prey Drive plays in your selling system, you must learn the three unique stages of selling: the Hit List, the Farm Club, and then finally the Red Zone. The Hit List identifies the prospects. The Farm Club is you working and cultivating the prospects to warm them up to your product or service. The Red Zone is the closing part of the cycle where prospects are ready to make a buying decision. Other components of the selling system to feed the system include the Showcase and the Top 25 strategy. The Showcase is you in front of people either online or in person showcasing your talents to them. The Top 25 strategy is you staying in a flow and frequency with your best clients and feeder systems to unlock new relationships and new opportunities for business.

Stage 1: The Hit List

In its essence, the Hit List represents people who you can help or people who can help you. Your Hit List consists of people who can help improve your skill set or help you advance toward a defining ambition. The goal of your Hit List is to find opportunities that can lead to new money.

Who should be on this list? Anyone who can help you advance your dreams or help generate revenue toward your dominant aspiration. I believe the future is collaborating and partnering with people. You don't need more money; you need more *people*. Because people have the money.

How do you get started with this list? You might start with current clients you want go deeper with and past clients you could engage with or offer additional products to; as well, both present and past clients might be able to introduce you to new strategic partners or even connect you to new opportunities or direct leads.

This Hit List is what will make your daily targets possible. Whether you are trying to sell $25,000 or collect $25,000 daily, that business has to come from somewhere. Use your Hit List to find that business, initiate new ways to solve problems for other people, and follow up on past ideas to bring potential buyers to a close and a sale.

Most of my days are spent calling on strategic partners to create a synergy between us and cross-pollinate our audiences. This results in connections to people that I'm not familiar with and may not be familiar with me; these are the people I call "new associations." New associations could be one person or ten thousand people. Whoever those associations are, you have to have something of value for them so you can bring them into your audience.

Once you are in front of these new audiences thanks to your Hit List, you will have the opportunity to showcase your specialty and generate more interest for your product or service. Remember, you don't need more money; you need more people, because people have the money. But those people will be of no value to your future enterprise unless you follow up with them and solve a problem or present an opportunity. This leads me to the Farm Club and the art of the follow-up.

Stage 2: The Farm Club

There are many rules to sales, but one in particular is more important than any other: *You must follow up.* That's where the Farm Club comes in.

The Farm Club represents all the people who have indicated interest in your product or service whom you have not closed. They have shown a level of interest, and now it's time for you to follow up with them to bring them to a close.

The follow-up is relevant to any opportunity that could open a door to a bigger future, not just a lead. People who have walked into your life and opened doors represent connections to others and connections to capital; these people can add some depth and relationship to your life and are all worth the follow-up.

There is never, and I mean *never*, a shortage of people or things to follow up with, including:

1. Dreams that you have and have had for years. (Why haven't you called the local university to inquire about its master's program?)
2. Relationships that matter to you. (Maybe you should congratulate your old colleague on LinkedIn when you see a notification about a work anniversary.)

3. Strategic partnerships with people who can advance your dreams. (How can you track down the person you met at the conference whom you admired and connected with?)

4. Key partners and advocates who continue to support you. (When was the last time you thanked or gestured appreciation to people who have been pivotal to your career journey thus far?)

5. Ideas you have that could help millions or make millions. (Did you do a comparative product or service analysis to see if there is a need for your idea?)

6. People who have capital. (How can you provide tangible materials to send to folks after you verbally pitched them?)

When following up on opportunity, it's important to know the real purpose of that follow-up, and this can include any of the following (and more):

- Solve a problem for another person.
- Help a person make a decision.
- Trigger a buying decision.
- Challenge the premise of the buyer or other person.
- Connect the dots for people who need new relationships to advance.
- Find a fear that is prohibiting a person from taking an action.

The purpose of your follow-up is to articulate the skill you possess that will solve your prospects' problems and help them make the decision to work with you. You have to (subtly) remind them that they need you. You are the *prize*.

The process of following up should consist of 7 to 15 follow-up touches that are both value touches (what I call "non-linear" or "indirect") and calls to action (what I call "linear" or "direct"). Why so many touches? The brain many times has to warm up to something, which is why it needs to see something, be comfortable with it, and have trust in the person who is sharing it before it will take an action to get involved. A value touch could be any of the following:

- An encouragement
- A strategy
- A testimonial
- A compliment
- A video

These touches give the prospect more information and more courage to make a decision. A direct touch would be a direct call to action if you believe the prospect is in the Red Zone and is ready to make a decision. With the direct touch you may ask a direct question to see if the person will move forward with an action. This is what represents the 7 to 15 touches, with 3 value touches for each direct touch. (I write about this in great detail in the book *Million Dollar Follow Up*.)

Stage 3: The Red Zone

This finally leads us to . . . the Red Zone, which is a term you may remember from Chapter 2. The term was inspired by the great college football coach Hugh Freeze. Red Zone people are those who are close to making a buying decision and require an outside force to make their final decision. *You will be this force.* You will come into their lives and bring the solution to solve their problem. You will articulate your value in such a compelling way that they will want to do business with you.

Red Zone people need one more piece of info, one more idea, one more strategy, or one different way of understanding how you will be an asset to them. And you have the confidence and Prey Drive to deliver exactly that.

Your job here is simple and mission critical—to follow up and give the other person or people what they need to make a key decision. When people are in the Red Zone, I use a series of direct comments to bring them to a close. These may include:

- "I can't help you until you commit, but once you commit, I'm not going to let you fail."
- "Have you seen enough to make a decision?"
- "It seems like you are ready to take action."
- "It feels like this is the perfect thing for you."
- "It sounds like you are ready to get started."
- "I'd like to bring this to a close for you."
- "All I'm trying to do is move you from A to B. Does this sound good to you?"

THE TOP 25: ALWAYS REMEMBER YOUR ADVOCATES

After I work my Hit List, my Farm Club, and my Red Zone, I then move to my Top 25, which represents 25 deep and meaningful relationships who can help me advance toward my dominant aspirations. These people are your advocates. They are the people who will fight for you in the marketplace, as long as you continue to support them in meaningful ways. These people have gone beyond promoters and are actively helping you expand your business by bringing new people to you in the form of prospects and referrals. There is mutual exchange and support here—these people add value to you just as much as you add value to them.

These 25 relationships fight for you. They advocate for you. They believe in you. They propel you. I believe that with the right Top 25, you can make millions of dollars per year.

The primary way I keep my Top 25 strong is to add some kind of unique value to them daily, weekly, monthly, and quarterly. This could be a text message, a phone call, or a value touch. Real value comes from bringing something positive to another and can be anything from an idea or a connection to a new association or new strategy. The key with the Top 25 is what I call "flow and frequency," meaning staying in a flow with these people and looking and listening to ways you can add unique value to their lives to help them advance. In essence, the best way is to get lost in their dreams.

People ask me all the time what they should be doing for these 25 relationships. I say one thing—*fight for them*. Ways you can do this include:

- Love them when they are down.
- Encourage them when they need you.
- Believe in them when they try something new.
- Get lost in their dreams.
- Help them move their ball down the field.
- Connect them to new and exciting opportunities.
- Bring clarity to their confusion and complexity.

I typically reach out to 3 of my top 25 per day. I'm there for them and constantly think about how I can help them move toward their B in life. My job is to bring them maximum value and put my arms around them for support.

Sit down right now and write out who would be in your Top 25. Do you actually have 25? If so, set a plan to stay in their lives and help them advance. If not, start by building just 5, and then keep expanding on the vision until you get to 25.

SHOWCASE TO SELL YOU

I finish off by always, and I mean *always*, planning a Showcase. A Showcase is an event that allows me to "show" my abilities and allows prospects to see me in action, because I know if they like what they see, they will want to buy more.

A Showcase could be a webinar or an in-person event. It could be a dinner, a conference, a concert, a sporting event. It could be for fun/entertainment, for education/learning, or for both! Whatever format you choose, the purpose of the event is to get in front of other people to show them your *special* and allow them to come to a conclusion that you can be of value to them.

Now I know what you might be thinking:

- "I don't know how to create something like this."
- "It will be hard."
- "It will take too long."
- "It will cost too much."
- "Nobody will come."

Those are all excuses. And ones I can easily dismantle. You don't have to spend a fortune to bring people together. An education meeting is a Showcase. A mastermind is a Showcase. Meeting up at a park is a Showcase.

The reality is, nothing motivates people or flips the switch to activate a person's Prey Drive more than being with other people who have the same energy, goals, and passions as you. Showcases are a great way to accomplish this, and if you do that for others, you will offer them tremendous value, no matter how big or small, complex or simple, your Showcase is.

There is *one* thing that has never led me wrong: bringing people together and allowing them to "exchange"—ideas, energy, money, or networks.

And I am always planning something in the future to push people toward their B and invite more people into our ecosystem. This is big. This keeps your prospects in a forward posture and serves to reignite your base of clients. Think of it as a great way to reignite the Prey Drive by bringing people together and "alerting them" to their future potential when they exchange with you. This process is an interesting way to instill a tremendous amount of confidence and Prey Drive not only in you, but in your team as well.

———

In his book *Deep Work*, Cal Newport gets into why people can be happier at work, drawing his ideas from the work of Mihaly Csikszentmihalyi, the psychologist most associated with flow state. In the book, Newport says: "Ironically, jobs are actually easier to enjoy than free time, because like flow activities, they have built-in goals, feedback rules, and challenges, all of which encourage one to become involved in one's work, to concentrate and lose oneself in it. Free time, on the other hand, is unstructured, and requires much greater effort to be shaped into something that can be enjoyed."[1]

The very cycle and movement of our selling system gets you into this flow state and allows you to use it. It's like Phil Jackson used the Triangle offense to bring structure but allow for creativity with the Bulls and Lakers. The Triangle offense was a series of actions that played off each other and could be used as a framework for the teams to read the competition and respond based on their readings. This increased the probability of multiple options that led to success.

Our selling system is very similar. It's a framework that can be utilized across multiple disciplines to drive up the probability of success. With each goal and expansion, the Prey Drive is activated to expand to greater and greater levels.

All of this makes up my Monster Growth System—a system that requires confidence, effort, persistence, and intensity. It's a system that requires a person to wake up every day and stay in the game at a high level rather than sitting on the sideline. Remember this: nothing happens until something is sold, and nothing is sold until you take an action to bring value to another person. The Prey Drive is in every single phase of the selling system and is what initiates the sales cycle.

WHAT WE LEARNED AND WHAT'S NEXT

To initiate the structure for selling, you will need a tremendous amount of Prey Drive and confidence and the necessary skills:

The Prey Drive initiates. This is making an outbound effort to communicate with your prospects about your product or service. You have an instinct, and you take an action to initiate a sale.

Confidence allows you to pursue with intensity. You know it is to the benefit of prospects to take action with you. You have a deep conviction that you can help others with your product or service and have removed any fear or consideration of failure, embarrassment, or rejection. You make the ask, and you allow your potential clients to respond.

Your skills allow you to articulate your value and bring something to a close. You work the deal until you have seen it through to its logical conclusion, meaning the prospects have taken an action to either buy or move on.

Once you have initiated the selling structure, you will generate more leads, which will need to be converted to actual clients. The faster you can see your work as the distribution of your talents to solve problems and enhance other people's lives, the faster this work can serve your Prey Drive so that it is activated over and over again.

In this chapter, we flipped the switch on selling. In the next chapter we flip the switch on your selling energy. We'll explore how much energy you have, what type of energy you exude, and how well you use it—how your energy affects your prospects.

 Watch Coach break down his entire selling system and get his seven top closes and conversions.

CHAPTER 8

Flipping the Switch on Your Selling Energy— and Beyond

Everything is energy and that's all there is to it.
—ALBERT EINSTEIN

As a salesperson, what are you really selling? Sure, you have to have a great product, but it's the type of *energy* you put behind the product, the reputation, and the company that's really responsible for closing the deal, not the conditions of the deal itself.

We are all made up of energy. The things we do, our gestures, our words, the rise and fall of our voices—all of it requires energy. Whether we know it or not, we pick up on people's energy and make unconscious decisions based on the feelings we have around a person. So it's safe to say that in selling, the right energy is the force behind the sale. Low energy = no sale; high energy . . . well, you get the idea. We naturally gravitate toward confidence, and then the money follows that energy. The question is, how much energy do you have, what type of energy do you exude, and how well do you use it?

What you are really selling is a sense of trust, conviction, power, and what I call a "future energy" that converts to action both on your part and on the part of the other person you are trying to elevate. Future energy is the energy you feel when you are around powerful people or those who exude an excitement about the future. It is that impression of increase we talked about in Chapter 5. What you are selling is a winning solution: Your customers will be in a better position in the future because they have a relationship with you. Your energy tells them . . .

- You are there to take care of them. This is not transactional, but rather transformational.
- You have valuable knowledge and a unique skill set that will help them achieve their goal and move them from A to B in a timely and caring manner.
- You have a demonstrated capacity to get the job done, and you have proved that over and over and over with other people and with yourself.
- You make them feel better about themselves, and you make them believe in their limitless opportunities. This ultimately is the impression of increase. Simply put, I feel better about me and my future when I'm with you.
- You are a person of advancement, meaning you are skilled at helping them advance toward their dreams and ambitions and away from their insecurities.
- You are a person that is moving, creating, and becoming more, and therefore others want to move, create, and become along with you. Remember, money follows movement and progress, not stagnation.

These messages embody the energy a high–Prey Drive person exudes. But many send messages of exhaustion. Those messages reflect isolation and helplessness, and that kind of energy doesn't garner support from others that you desperately need in order to advance.

There is a lost art of selling in our society because somewhere along the way selling has gotten a bad name. Sales is the art of getting another person excited about taking an action, following up until you have a conversion, and painting a bigger future through the product or service. All of this takes a high degree of energy.

Rate yourself on a scale of 1 to 10 on how much energy you bring to a sale. Do you get people excited, or do you allow them to stay in a static position? The high–Prey Drive person has high levels of certainty and confidence and utilizes those to make a sale.

DRAIN OR GAIN? WHAT'S YOUR ENERGY DOING?

I like to define energy as "a means or source for supplying energy to others." When you hear people who are attracted to powerful people, they are just attracted to people who are supplying energy to others. Are you a powerful energy source to those around you, propelling them further, showing them you are contender, and making them see they can become one, too? Or are you an energy drain, a pretender whose low or negative energy doesn't influence or inspire, leaving people underwhelmed?

How can you tell? Low-energy people, especially in sales, give off a negative energy of being closed, nontrusting, or passionless; they seem disconnected, just going through the motions.

Salespeople who exude a positive attitude show an openness to connect with others and solve their problems. Remember, there is a correlation between money and problem solving. When you have an energy that says you've come to do business, business gets done. You walk in with an *energy of increase*. You display to the other people that you are here to help and not hurt. You bring a confidence about you that radiates. You walk in with your head up and your shoulders back. You are warm and connecting and inviting.

I once coached a mortgage advisor who struggled to connect with others and was underperforming. I observed that he gave off a nervous energy that made him difficult to connect with. He asked me one day why I thought he wasn't advancing, and I shared that I thought the nervous energy he generated created distance between him and others. It was hard to calculate, but you could feel it. Instead of taking that feedback as a learning opportunity, he got offended and quit the coaching program. This is an example of a closed mindset versus an open mindset. I couldn't help him with his bad energy because he wouldn't accept feedback (even though he asked for some).

On the opposite side of things, I've also coached people who weren't that great at selling, but they created an incredible energy that others felt and wanted more of. These people would show up to coaching assignments, meet and mingle with others, demonstrate strong support for others, and make meaningful business connections. They would then use the selling system to follow up and close deals. They came back to me later and said that within just eight months in our programs, they had secured over $800,000 of new business due to our networks.

How many times have you been involved with groups of people and you always showed up with the same energy and talked to the same people? But you never met new people, never identified problems, and never followed up until you had a deal. Your energy was not fully activated. Selling is a full-contact sport of meeting and greeting, building and forging strong relationships, finding and solving problems, and seeing things through to their logical conclusions.

In Chapter 1, I spoke about the work of Dr. Stephen Covey, who introduced the concept of tending to the "whole person"—body, mind, heart, and spirit. When it comes to providing a consistent message and experience in your sales relationships, it is helpful to consider whether what you are saying, selling, and doing taps into each part of a person to speak to the whole person. In turn, are you selling *with* your whole person? Doing this requires you to sell with your full knowledge, skills, desires, and confidence. Your solutions to people's confusion, isolation, and powerlessness is to bring a high level of direction, connection, and new and improved creativity to their problems. Do your body, mind, heart, and spirit participate equally in your selling? If they do, that means your energy is in full activation, setting you up for maximum results.

Your energy is attached to your attitude. The more your attitude comes from all the parts of yourself, the better your attitude and the better your energy. Attitude shows in the posture of the body. You give off signals to others by how you present yourself physically, with your posture reflecting your good or bad energy. This is why body language is everything in sales—both yours and your prospects'. Many times you know within 15 to 30 seconds of making your offer if others are interested in your product or service by their attitude and body language:

Some exude difficulty (they walk in late) and have a closed posture.

Some exude distance (they position their chair slightly askew from yours).

Some exude happiness (they make eye contact and smile genuinely) and bring a good energy into the room.

Some exude defensiveness (they talk with their arms or legs crossed) and seem skeptical.

Some exude scarcity (they always bring up why something may not work).

What kind of energy and attitude do you put out?

On one of my episodes on the podcast *Flip the Switch*, I talked about a sermon by Jimmy Evans, a straight-talking pastor from Amarillo (you may remember my mentioning him earlier in the book). In his sermon he explained the concept of "attitude indicators" that are in the cockpit of a plane. These instruments indicate whether the plane is:

- Ascending—heading up, moving, advancing
- Plateaued—static or moving in a straight line, stuck, or plateaued
- Descending—coming in for a landing, headed in a downward position

Using this idea as a starting point, I've created my own "attitude indicators," which go like this:

- Dynamic—alive, growing, pursuing, and interested
- Static—stuck, complacent, bored, and in a rut
- Declining—indicating a negative or downward spiral

Where do you think you fall?

ATTITUDE ASSESSMENT

To adjust our attitudes, we first need to assess them. Assessments require honesty. Take a close look at your daily interactions, and consider what kind of attitude you are possibly exuding. Based on my experience, I've identified three types of people:

1. **THOSE WHO ARE NOT INTERESTED IN THEIR POTENTIAL OR ARE NOT EVEN AWARE THEY CAN GET BETTER.** They have lost hope and belief even in the idea of a better life. Many are simply ignorant of a better way because they have never been exposed to a better way. This is why exposure is such an important activator of the Prey Drive. *When I know better, I do better.*

2. **THOSE WHO REACH A LEVEL OF SUCCESS AND BECOME LAZY OR COMPLACENT.** I believe lazy and complacent are two distinct paths. Lazy people let their weight get out of control. Complacent people have a prevent mindset, which means they are playing defense in life and allowing themselves to plateau out in an area of life—and know it; they actually know they are slipping.

3. **THOSE WHO ARE HUMBLE, HUNGRY, CURIOUS, AND TEACHABLE.** These are the folks looking for a better way of life and are open to change; they are vulnerable and ready to mix it up. (These are my people.)

You have to decide which of these you currently are and who you are going to be.

Here are some key questions that will help you determine if you are open to new growth or if you have a fixed mindset:

1. Are you currently satisfied with where you are, or would you like to find a better, more profitable way to conduct life and business?
2. When was the last time you invested in your own personal growth and development in an area of your life?
3. How long have you allowed yourself to become stuck and static in your current position, and are you OK with that position?
4. Are you ready to get in the game of personal and business development to get to some new levels of success in life?

When it comes to assessing the attitude you have right now about your life and business, here are few questions to do an attitude check. Are you:

- Actively promoting your product or service on a frequent basis? Or has this become a drain on your energy and been affecting your attitude?
- Making outbound efforts to become known to the world and get people excited to take action on your product or service?
- Getting in front of new people to find and solve problems?
- Following up like crazy to stay consistent and bring real solutions?
- Working to close deals with people who are in your Red Zone and Farm Club?
- Servicing and engaging your clients to increase their lifetime value, and are you seeking to initiate referrals?
- Working to collect money that is owed to your company that may not have come in yet?

These would all be positive indicators of your attitude that you are actively engaged with your business versus disengaged. Disengaged entrepreneurs allow the wear and tear of running the business to place them in a negative state and beat the life and positive attitude out of them. This is why you need people and structures to support your vision and execute on your vision, so you do not run into this burned-out state. Burnout is a loss of all joy or passion for something, and when you get in this state, it negatively affects everything in the business. The Prey Drive is no longer there; it has been suppressed to the point of being nonexistent. This is particularly hard on small businesses. Owing to the margins and volume of the business, small businesses simply can't sustain these down periods because there is no cushion. During this cycle, many small businesses move into a downward spiral that gets out of control and ultimately causes them to fold or be sold at a discounted price.

BAD ATTITUDE BE GONE

Bad-attitude thinkers set themselves up for failure and negativity. For these kinds of people, when one thing doesn't go their way, their initial response is to blame others, quit, or complain. Instead, they should be thinking:

"What did I do to create this scenario?"

"What was my contribution to this?"

"Could I have spoken up?"

"Could I have prepared better?"

The high–Prey Drive person doesn't whine, complain, or make excuses. Good-attitude thinkers know they don't have to complain about a negative experience or have a negative attitude along the way. They realize there's an opportunity for learning and growth and use that experience to set themselves up for success the next time.

Whether you are a bad-attitude thinker or a good-attitude thinker, having a strategy to approach adversity can help you. Here is a simple five-step strategy I use when I have to deal with an adverse situation:

1. I make up my mind that everything is a gain and there is neither a positive nor a negative connotation to it.
2. I ask myself, "What was my contribution to this adversity?"
3. I replace the question, "Why me?" with "What is this trying to teach me?"
4. I get help from someone who has been there and done that.
5. I get busy. When in doubt, take an action toward a desired outcome. Don't marinate in the past. Get moving with the new knowledge of what didn't work.

Take personal responsibility for your own attitude, and don't worry about others.

STATIC ENERGY LEVEL BE GONE!

If your energy is static, meaning it's not moving up or down, you're in the most insidious and dangerous state of energy. Why? Because you've become complacent. Your basic needs are met. You feel a sense of that false positive that leads you to believe you will always stay in this position with no threat of losing what you have. This is the greatest suppressor for your Prey Drive and is contrary to what characterizes the high–Prey Drive person.

Remember, the high–Prey Drive person:

1. Goes to bed tired and wakes up hungry
2. Knows and believes it all goes to zero at midnight (whether it does or not)
3. Knows it will be a fight and expects trials and tribulations
4. Knows there comes a time when winter asks what you did all spring and summer

The Prey Drive is what reminds you that you don't have to be average. In life there are two options: grow or wither away. Like a house plant that is forgotten and taken for granted, without water and sunlight (and even a human to talk to it once in a while), it will begin to wither, and finally, if not resuscitated in time, will die. Dynamic people are those who have made a decision to nurture themselves and look for the Prey Drive activators they know help them answer their Because Goals. They are hungry, humble, coachable. And when they feel they are waning, they identify their suppressors and seek out activators to reengage their Prey Drive and drive their energy and attitudes toward the positive.

Some signs that you may be allowing yourself to become static with your energy could be:

1. You are not working on your physical self or your energy levels.
2. You have plateaued in your business and career goals.
3. It has been a while since you have placed yourself in situations for growth.

4. You are not routinely working on the A to B exercise.
5. You secretly know that you have more to give, and yet you allow yourself to fall into complacency.

The reason we become static is simple: we give up. Our self-image is too low. We give up on making it big. We give up on how we look. We give up on our dreams and goals. We give up on our relationships. We give up on our drive. We end up stuck in the static position.

And what will likely be even harder to hear is the longer you stay in that static position, the faster you get into a declining position, which means disintegrating and dying. The antidote is to get back in a dynamic position. How do you do that? By doing things that replenish your soul and activate and reactivate your drive, such as:

- Start your day with a moment of gratitude and celebration.
- Structure a big win.
- Create a major impact.
- Look back at the progress you've made.
- Focus on the gains in your life versus always the gap (a Dan Sullivan and Benjamin Hardy concept).
- Engage in a healthy competition or with a good nemesis.

You know yourself best, so be sure to make your own list of what activates and reactivates you, and be sure to revisit that list anytime you feel yourself getting static or stagnant.

I like to remind my nine-year-old daughter that "bad attitudes make for hard lives" because bad attitudes cause us to lose the support we need from others. Make a decision today that you're going to flip the switch on your attitude and on your energy so that you can experience greater and greater levels of rewards and satisfaction.

WHAT WE LEARNED AND WHAT'S NEXT

At the end of the day, each of us is in control of our energy. That energy is either open and inviting or closed to new possibilities. After all the work we've done in this chapter, you likely know where your energy falls: dynamic, static, or declining.

The work we do in the next chapter will help you use your Prey Drive to hit your targets.

 Watch Coach Burt's course on *The Art of Making MONEY.*

CHAPTER 9

Hitting Your Targets

Using the Prey Drive to Structure Your Success and Go Pro

You miss 100% of the shots you don't take.
—WAYNE GRETZKY

While I was sitting at a coffee shop many years ago, a good friend of mine named Tony Woodall told me he had just read an article in *Fast Company* about a zebra and a cheetah. He said: "You know, Coach, a zebra looks different than every other animal in the animal kingdom, and a cheetah runs faster than every other land animal. The goal in life is to look different and run faster." A zebra is clearly differentiated from the rest of the animal kingdom. A cheetah runs faster and is usually on offense in the savanna versus on defense. In the business world it's always a good idea to look different and run faster than your competitors.

When he mentioned the concept, I said, "Bingo!" and a talented writer named Colby Jubenville and I went on to write the book *Zebras and Cheetahs*.

As I prepared to work on that book, I studied the cheetah; I was most interested in its intensity. This beautiful animal has a closing ratio of over 60 percent, meaning that it sees its prey, pursues it, and captures it six times out of ten. On top of that, the cheetah is so intense that if it doesn't kill its prey within a concentrated period, it might turn that instinct on itself. Therefore, it has to calm itself down in order to control the natural instinct it has to kill itself. If business were a hunting ground, would you be pursuing and initiating deals that create revenue as if your life depended on it?

In Chapter 2 we discussed moving from A to B. Point A is the current position you are in, and Point B is the target; it's what you shoot for. Too many people let time pass and one day wake up regretful they never pursued their B, but instead allowed life to keep them at A. Unlike the cheetah, these people have given up—they continue to stay where they are rather than pursue their bigger futures.

Who hasn't heard of the person who has written the great American novel that sits in a drawer? Or the master class that never gets taken, or the online networking that never occurs? The intensity of the Prey Drive enables us to see something through to its logical conclusion, like the cheetah catching its prey.

Speaking of the cheetah, intensity is not the only element here that makes that cat such a wondrous thing to watch. The cheetah is not erratic about closing in on its prey. That intensity has a structure to it, a pointed reason, a game plan that keeps the cheetah in control. The cheetah knows what it wants. That's clarity. As applied to us humans, clarity is a way to filter what you are going after. I start every day by looking at those opportunities that are biggest to me (my Level 10 opportunities) and by going over my list of Blue Marlins. Blue Marlins are those people who can help you move from A to B with their influence and networks. Blue Marlins are the big fish who introduce you to new associations and new people, and as I said earlier in the book, you don't need more money—you need more people. The people always have the money. Blue Gills, on the other hand . . . well, these are the small fish.

For years I felt like I was a Level 10 person, but I was stuck at what I'd call Level 4 opportunities. When this is the case, it means you are highly capable of more, but you're not focusing on your Level 10 opportunities (the biggest opportunities available to you right now) because you're too busy keeping things going and fishing for Blue Gills. My goal is to set targets and not waiver from them; that means applying pressure on all the people who are attached to that goal so they will see it through to its conclusion.

Just as a cheetah sets its sights on prey to eat at the end of the day, you must set not only your sales targets but your timeline. Giving yourself 10 years to become a top earner in your company will get you nowhere and mean nothing, because you are not setting an immediate standard against which to measure yourself. There has to be a standard, a quantitative target to know if you are winning or losing.

If you don't hit your targets, ask yourself whether you are structured like a cheetah, going straight for your prey. Or are you going out into the wild, unfocused and hunting for whatever comes across your path—which isn't hunting at all.

WHERE IS YOUR MISSING STRUCTURE?

Anytime you are behind in reaching your target, it typically comes down to an issue that in our coaching business we call a "missing structure." A missing structure is a gap or hole in your business mindset or model. Saying your issue is a missing structure is a softer way of saying you have a problem.

When people are not hitting targets in their lives, it is usually because one or more of the following structures are missing:

1. **KNOWLEDGE.** Will you invest to get in the room to gain the knowledge needed to deliver what your client needs and meet your goals? Most of the time it will require a financial investment if you want to garner new knowledge. It will come via studying privately with someone, going to a conference, or investing in courses. Don't be cheap in your thoughts when it comes to investing in your learning. This learning will help you move from A to B because you have a new knowledge set.

2. **SKILL.** Sometimes people lack the talent or ability to achieve the mission and target. I believe money doesn't buy you freedom, but rather skills buy you freedom. Skills are a result of repetition, role play, and testing, and your primary skills are what will help you solve a problem in the world. Once you identify a primary skill, you can refine it over a cycle of time until that skill becomes incredibly valuable.

3. **DESIRE.** Many people simply don't have the discipline to achieve the mission and target. Lack of discipline usually means they lack the Prey Drive necessary to

advance. I start most of my coaching focused on desire, because if desire is lacking, nothing else matters.

4. **CONFIDENCE.** Not possessing the self-assurance to see a project through to its conclusion is sometimes the culprit that keeps you stuck where you are. Whether people waiver when there is adversity or utilize their confidence to see the project through makes a difference. It takes a remarkable boldness to fight through the toughness of the world to achieve a target.

5. **RELATIONSHIPS.** Many times, people lack access to others who can help them advance their dreams from A to B. This is an indicator that you are not placing yourself in key positions to be around the right people. Successful, powerful people recognize talent and attitude in others. But if you don't get in the room, you can't be recognized—and without recognition you can't form new relationships.

6. **REMARKABLE BOLDNESS.** "Boldness" is synonymous with words like "bravery," "daring," "courage," "determination," "adventurousness," and "audacity." When you add the adjective "remarkable," which the *Oxford English Dictionary* defines as "worthy of attention; striking," the implication is a special kind of boldness that draws on the attention of others.

Another missing structure could be the lack of intensity to take ideas and see them through to their conclusion or bring them to a close. Think of the last time that you really wanted something. Did time matter to you? Did obstacles matter to you? Were you willing to accept excuses in this scenario, or did you move toward what you wanted with a sense of urgency? Intensity is what moves you from A to B at a faster clip. Utilizing intensity with a structure and a timeline expedites the cycle.

For many people, this mindset of intensity is what is missing. They operate without a sense of urgency, as if they have all the time in the world. But in reality, our time on Earth is fleeting.

Imagine if you began to look at how many actual days you had left on Earth from where you are now. According to the most recent data available from the Centers for Disease Control and Prevention, the average life expectancy in the United States is *78.6 years*—76.1 years for men and 81.1 years for women. When you calculate just how much more time you may have left on Earth, it really shows you that *now* is the time to make the impact you want.

Many years ago, I put the number "18,000" on the whiteboard in my office. Then I called the members of my team together and asked them what they thought it meant. Some guessed revenue, some thought it was the number of clients I wanted, and some said sales goal. I replied, "No, this represents the number of days I have left on Earth should I live to be 84 years old. I have a long way to go to accomplish what I want to accomplish and a short time to get there." I explained to the people on my team that if they experienced an intensity from me, it was for this reason. Think *big* goals and *short* runways. This is part of what characterizes the high–Prey Drive person: going to bed tired and waking up hungry.

Let's go back to earlier in the book when we created our Tired of Messing Around List. By creating that list and highlighting things you are ready to get off the fence, you have already created some of the fire and focus that you need. The next two questions help bring even more fire and focus. Add your answers to your list.

1. What are the top three projects you need to bring to a close? When would you like these to be finalized?
2. What are the three biggest messes/headaches you want to remove from your plate to free up your mental space and increase your happiness?

To keep from being casual about your future, laser-focus on your Tired of Messing Around List.

———

The world rewards action. It never rewards stagnation. Creating intensity is about creating a target and understanding that your number one goal is "compressing time" toward that target—whether that's counting the 18,000 days you might have left or waking up every day with an understanding that the hours and minutes must count. That takes planning. It takes strategy. It also takes ferocity and remarkable boldness. The Prey Drive is the instinct to pursue, not sit and wait. There are moments in life that wake us up out of our slumber and prompt us to go from complacency to consistency, to want more. Our goal should not be to wait for something to prompt us, but rather to learn how to prompt ourselves through learning these Prey Drive activation techniques.

When setting goals for the days, months, and years ahead, I have always believed that "Done is better than perfect." So many people get sidetracked focusing on perfecting every detail or getting opinions about how and what they are doing. For example, I've seen people spend their time working on a single problem or arguing over who was right (or smarter). It's the people with intensity who are focused on the end result that accomplish the target. Until you develop an intensity about you, and strategize with that intensity using definite goals and deadlines, others with a higher drive will continue to run circles around you.

People consistently ask me what separates the top performers from others in my coaching program. I always give them the same answer: "The top performers come and learn and go and do. From the time of concept to execution, there is an intensity about action. In the end this is the separation point."

Can this level of intensity be developed? It's a worthy question. I refer again to Steven Kotler in *The Art of Impossible*, when he wrote: "Over the past fifty years, when scientists turn their attention to excellence and achievement, three factors have played an outsized role: mothers, musicians, and marshmallows."[1]

Mothers reflect the nature and nurture side of the equation. Genetics and early childhood environments are crucial for learning and success. My mother instilled an intensity in me early in life due to her intensity. We dress up, we grow up, we show up, and we deliver. We don't whine, we don't complain, and we don't make excuses. We are people of interest in the world, and there is no excuse for not getting things done. Everything else is just that, an excuse. Even to this day my own mother will call me out on my excuses when I utilize them.

Musicians are an allusion to the violinists that Anders Ericsson studied when he came up with his idea of "deliberate practice" to generate the 10,000 hours of success formula. I believe this 100 percent. My high school team won a championship in the tenth year I had been coaching. And it was in the tenth year of my business when we had major breakthroughs. The great musicians put in the work, get the coach, receive the feedback, and perform over and over. They are critical of their own performance and are always working to make it better.

They compete, and when they do, the competition encourages them to strive and push toward bigger targets.

Marshmallows are a reference to Stanford psychologist Walter Mitchell's experiment in delayed gratification. Mitchell found that children who could resist temptation in the present moment—eating a marshmallow now—for the promise of a bigger reward—getting two marshmallows later—were far more successful in life. I believe that discipline is the ability to subordinate what you want now for what you want eventually. The ability to work through challenges and continue to chop wood and carry water daily toward a dominant aspiration and activate and reactivate your drive is critical to your long-term success. This delayed gratification is tough on the intensity, which is why you need the other piece of the Prey Drive, persistence. Remember, the three phases of the Prey Drive have to work in harmony to move toward the defining ambition. The Prey Drive must be activated. It must have a persistence. And there must be an intensity. All three pushing and working together is the intersection of greatness.

All of this relates to how intense you are:

- Do you go for it, or do you make excuses?
- Do you compress time, and when you think of something, do you take action on it?
- Do you get caught up in the mechanics of how something is going to get done, or do you dream it and take action toward manifesting it into reality?

Are your goals big enough to activate that drive and get you moving? *People with small goals have little intensity.*

Adopt the Mindset and Action of a Cheetah

Let's go back to the concept of the cheetah and the fact that this animal is always on offense. What mindset and actions would a cheetah use each day in the workplace? I think the cheetah would attack a day like this:

- Stay in creation mode, knowing there is no shortage or lack, only abundance.
- Create opportunity by locating problems and attacking those problems.
- Focus on who can help it move from A to B.
- Go deep into strategic relationships because, remember, we don't need more money; we need more people. The Top 25 strategy is a place the cheetah starts to work and massage key relationships with people who have access to more people. This implies that you have developed and nurtured 25 deep and meaningful relationships with people who believe in you, and you believe in them. These healthy relationships grow and build, and these people introduce you to others, producing a never-ending cycle of new opportunities for you.
- Diversify income profit centers. When one stream is not working, open another door, or come to market in another way, so as not to allow one ineffective stream to prohibit other successes.
- Go for the close when the opportunity presents itself. Cheetahs ask direct questions and understand there is no sale until there is a close. They perfect the closing technique and learn the art of overcoming the objection to bring another to a decision. Objection in the sales cycle is opposition of thought and can be overcome through certainty. This certainty comes from

a demonstrated capacity of doing something over and over and over.

- Expand its goals to activate and reactivate that Prey Drive, and never rest on past wins.
- Refocus on connection to others, knowing this is the secret sauce to closing. Closing is really just helping others locate a real problem they want to solve and showing them that you have the real (and best) solution to that problem

MOVING FROM CASUAL TO PRO

My wife and I recently took our daughter, a gymnast, to a Level 10 coach. She had been operating at what some would call a "casual level." She practices and studies gymnastics on her own daily. She also desires to go pro but doesn't know what pro looks like. At the time I signed her up with the Level 10 coach, the coach told me, "Before she comes, please let her know that the girls she will be performing with practice four days per week for four hours. They are serious and have been well conditioned to the kind of toughness it really takes to go pro. She may feel lost or confused or not be used to working at this pace, and we want her to be prepared for this."

"This is exactly what she needs," I responded.

To first go *pro*, you have to see, be exposed to, the lifestyle of a pro, and understand what it takes to operate at that pro level. Once you see it, you have to make an internal decision of whether or not you are willing to go there and what the benefits are if you do so. My good friend Dr. Elko says, "Some people play football on Friday night. Some play on Saturday. But only the pros play on Sunday." And to take that a step further, only champions play in the Super Bowl. Only you can decide what level you are going to play at.

My first exposure to a pro came when I was 18. Division II basketball coach Don Meyer was hosting free coaching clinics, and I didn't miss even one. I sat in the front row and took notes like crazy, watching and activating everything he said. At 25 I flew to Boston to sit at the feet of my motivational master, Dr. Stephen Covey. My own mother tracked down his personal assistant so I could get just 10 minutes privately with him. That one meeting changed my life and opened my dreams to bigger possibilities. Since that time, I've worked my way into relationships with Ed Mylett, Tim Grover, Tim Storey, Grant Cardone, Brad Lea, Sharon Lechter, and many other key influencers. Each has deposited important knowledge, skill, desire, and confidence in me and changed my life forever.

If I were giving you a formula to get in the room with a real pro, it would be this:

1. Create a real skill and talent that others would recognize and find valuable.
2. Deliver consistently on what you promise.
3. Go where the pros are. Quit making excuses that it's not the right time or you don't have the money to get in the room.
4. Get in a flow and frequency with the pros.
5. Find a way to add significant value to these people.

It is also vitally important that when you have studied under someone, you must actually apply what you learn. I can't tell you how many people have come up to me and told me that they volunteered to work Tony Robbins events. I say, "Great, what are you doing with what you learned under Tony?" Many times they say, "Nothing."

It doesn't matter how many events you usher or attend if you don't *internalize*, *synthesize*, and *take action* on what you learned. Too many people are interested in implementing a quick fix versus doing the deep work to really master the content and begin utilizing it to improve their skill sets. Focus on the long term and the deep work, and that's how you'll achieve lasting and meaningful success.

As we bring this chapter to an end, I want to ask some great questions to help you assess where you are in relationship to the intensity levels it takes to go pro in your sales career:

1. Do you set and achieve targets, and if not, are you ready to start?
2. Do you compress time and add pressure to yourself daily? Tim Grover says, "Pressure is a privilege."
3. Do you create a new game to play, a new trophy to win, and place yourself around people who compete to draw out the best in you?
4. Is there any part of your life that you could say you are truly intense about?
5. Are there any consequences when you don't hit the targets you set for yourself that would cause you to change your behavior and take them more seriously?

WHAT WE LEARNED AND WHAT'S NEXT

Remember that the Prey Drive is an instinct to pursue. This chapter has been about pursuing deals and hitting your targets. How you handle the various components of the sales cycle could be the difference in millions of dollars of new revenue for you. Stay focused on finding and filling in your key missing structures and moving from casual to pro.

In the next chapter, we'll work together to prioritize and personalize your Prey Drive.

 Watch Coach Burt's video *Going Pro* and see the difference between amateurs and professionals.

CHAPTER 10

Prioritizing and Personalizing Your Prey Drive

The Keys to Continued Expansion

If what you did yesterday seems big,
you haven't done anything today.

—LOU HOLTZ

As Tim Grover wrote in *Winning*, "The greats celebrate for less than 30 seconds and then they are on to their next win."[1] I'll be the first to admit, I've never been good at celebrating. When I was interviewing to be the youngest head coach in the state of Tennessee at the second-largest high school at the age of 22, I was asked by the principal why he should hire me when there were clearly many other people more qualified. He pushed all the résumés of the other coaches across the table and told me it was not logical to hire someone as young as me. Without hesitation I said: "I'll do something no other coach has been able to do. I'll bring you a championship gold ball and ring." *It was a Prey Drive moment!*

It would take me 10 years to win that gold ball and a sacrifice of almost everything, but I did it. After I retired, the school would go on to win seven more championships in the next nine years, and I'm prouder of that than winning the first one. Why? Because that was a legacy to me. The night we won a championship, I took the gold ball around town with me as I tried to find a place to celebrate after all the press interviews.

In the end, a burger with fries at Steak 'n Shake and a few mixed drinks at a rundown bar at the Clarion with my new girlfriend and the gold ball beside me was my celebration. It was perfect, and I soaked in that night and every emotion it brought. And in the morning I was ready to move on to my next big play. I was already bored with an achievement that took me *10 years* to win.

I can't tell you how many successful people I coach feel the same way. They have pursued and pursued and pursued and finally captured—and almost immediately feel ready for a new challenge. The problem is, many don't have clarity on what that next challenge actually is.

What these successful people are experiencing is *hunger.* That hunger that comes with a pursuit is what drives successful people. But when that pursuit ends, it's easy for people to become complacent or bored, hit ceilings, or stagnate. The key here is to replace the old hunger with a new hunger, to replace the old trophies with some new desires. When you accomplish one big feat, you then need to reactivate the Prey Drive by adding a new challenge to the equation. This serves to expand and excite and get you ready to tackle something new. The continued expansion to new and bigger goals serves as an expansion of the Prey Drive and won't allow us to become comfortable with yesterday's trophies.

Too many people do something big one time and then spend the rest of their lives reliving that moment. These people are no longer hungry. And they've lost their Prey Drive. It's the dad who was an all-state football player who relives his glory days at his son's Friday night games. It's the sales manager who had a good sales career only to gloat around the office about when he used to be in the game. Are you still living with your old championships? Sure, I refer to what I *learned* during that decade of winning a championship, but I don't live in it. I have new wins to focus on—and you need that, too.

The top performers in the world are most motivated by the thrill of the chase. It's the pursuit of their potential that gets them excited, not capturing the reward. There is something inside of you that knows this and wants you to reach your maximum potential.

When I was 27 years old, a neighbor of mine informed me about an "Achiever's Circle" led by a gentleman named Mark Leblanc. Mark was a small business expert and came to town several times a year with his three-day boot camp. He was so good. He outlined tactics and strategy to start, grow, and build a business, and his teachings were practical and valuable. As part of the experience, he forced each of us in the room to identify our "optimistic number"—the number we wanted to hit in a 30-day cycle. The person beside me said $80,000. The person on the other side said $180,000. I said a measly $5,000. I said to the group, "If I could just hit $5,000 per month in extra income and marry that with my basketball coaching income, I would be earning $100,000 per year, and it would change my life." That was my target at that point in my life. It's all I could see to get to $100,000 of personal income. Now that number is exponentially higher.

Many people hit a target, and then they give up and call it a day. They make the $100,000 a month like me and say they've done what they wanted. But you have the potential for so much more. You have the potential to surpass your starting goals—but you have to set bigger targets. You have to set targets that get you excited and motivated to get out of bed in the morning.

A new person joined our team a year or two ago in the sales department and came from a large well-known company. Talented and hungry, he came in with a tendency to make a few sales for the day and then call it quits and go home. I noticed and asked him what he was doing. He said, "At my previous company, when we hit our quota for the day, we were done."

I said, "Things are different here. When you hit your target here, you keep going." We live by a certain set of principles. *We go to bed tired, and we wake up hungry. It all goes to zero at midnight.* We don't "shut it down" for the day when we hit our goal. We accelerate toward a bigger one. This was merely a habit in the old culture.

What are your habits when you achieve a goal? Do you allow that goal to be your only goal, or do you find new goals to work toward?

The greats win and quickly go for other wins. The amateurs win and rest.

USE YOUR STUCK TO SIGNAL THE PREY DRIVE

At 31, I was tired. I was frustrated. I had done everything I could possibly do at the school where I worked, and I loved every minute of it until then. I'm sure many of you have been there, too.

Tired, frustrated, exhausted, and bored. My heart and mind told me there was a bigger future for me. The problem was, I wasn't quite sure what that next play was. I just knew I needed to move toward a bigger opportunity. I, like so many others, *felt like I was a Level 10 person stuck at a Level 4 opportunity.*

Then, at a banquet where I was hired to give a speech for less than $250, a gentleman approached me from the back of the room and gave me an affirmation that would change my life and open my mind to new and exciting possibilities. He validated the potential in me for what would become my next Level 10 opportunity. It was after I gave my speech that he came up to me and said, "Son, you're good, and you could do this all over the world on the circuit."

I asked him what circuit he was referring to. And he said, "The speaking circuit." And then he said, "Like Lou Holtz." Those were the magic words. Lou Holtz was the famous football coach of the Notre Dame Fighting Irish. The gentleman had lit a fire in me to learn more. I immediately went home that night and began to search for Lou Holtz videos, and this would inspire me to want to speak, train, and write books for people around the world.

So I set a goal of starting my business, and from there, the next goal was just trying to survive, like so many others. I didn't have an explanation of value or even understand what a story of origin was. I didn't have a selling system. I didn't have a follow-up plan. I didn't have a way to get referrals from my current clients or expand my networks. I didn't have anything. All I had was grit, confidence, and a desire to play at a much higher frequency. So I took my energy out to the market every day, and eventually good things happened. Remember, money follows movement. My phone began to ring. Referrals began to come in. The Showcase strategy I used to get in front of people started to pay off. All I had was energy, but I was sharing that energy with so many, that something good was bound to happen.

It wasn't until I got coaching from some of the best in the world that I understood the concept of moving toward an optimistic number, which was a tangible number I was trying to create in a 30-day cycle. Once I learned and identified that, I had a new championship to win and a new game to play. Without a target, boredom sets in. The target should be used to excite us, move us, inspire us. The idea of a future outcome that pulls us toward it should get us up in the morning and keep us up at night. If the target (our B) is too small, then we lull into complacency and lack the persistence and intensity we need to fulfill it.

Surpassing your goals is ultimately all about expansion. It's about a mindset of expansion as opposed to one of contraction. It's about scaling up versus playing small.

Dr. Stephen Covey always talked about the difference between a rise and the summit. When climbing a mountain, you reach several rises. This is where you can see more now than you ever have or could before. It is not the top though, because there is always another much higher. In life, this is how you keep going. You keep climbing, and each step of the way you come to your rise en route to the next summit.

For me, my summits appear as setting and achieving some kind of monthly financial target for the company, then assessing how we did it, and then trying to replicate it at least three months in a row. If that goal is accomplished, I raise the target. This keeps us in an upward spiral of growth and improvement, and I never face stagnation. The target is the rise, not the summit. It's also important here to remember that gap that we live in that both motivates and frustrates us. There is an art for the high achievers to find happiness in the pursuit of the prey while simultaneously not losing their fight.

LET YOUR WORK FEED YOUR LIFE

With that constant pursuit of the next summit, there is quite a bit of sacrifice, which is a concept I think a lot about. I believe sacrifice is the giving up of something to get something greater. In so many cases, people sacrifice everything to get to great. But it doesn't have to be that way. I've come to believe in more of an intentionally congruent life where the business supports the life versus engulfs the life. In an ideal world the business is there to serve your life and not run your life, but it must be structured in a new way for this to happen; and you will need the help of key players and support staff to build the company around your unique skill sets.

From ages 18 to 31, I sacrificed a lot personally. I missed out on so many things, such as key relationships, the normal things a 20-something does, and depth with my closest family members due to my intense drive to be a championship coach. This drive superseded everything in my life and totally consumed me. I had few friends, virtually no hobbies, and only one driving ambition, which was to win. From 31 to 38, I was so intent on building my business that I lost friends, I was disconnected from the world, and I was on the road and away from my family more than I was with them. From 38 to 44, I've came to understand that work can *fuel* life. It can *enhance* life. And most important, it doesn't have to *consume* life.

Today I include my family in my work. I take my daughter on the road with me. My wife and I do couples retreats together. We even created Success School for Kids that our own kids participate in. This is intentional congruence at the highest levels where everything feeds everything in an intentionally congruent manner.

I believe (and finally see) that we *can* have it all. I see a clear way that in order to pursue my work goals, I have to do that alongside the goals of my family. Although this may not be balance, it can be intentionally congruent. This congruence of doing what you love doing—the things in life that both fascinate and motivate you—and taking time with and including your family and friends in what you are doing: this is what restimulates the Prey Drive for more and more expansion. You are no longer overwhelmed by your commitments but fueled by them.

WHAT WE LEARNED AND WHAT'S NEXT

It is critical to go for whatever lights a fire in you to learn more, whatever inspires you. The idea is to continually surpass your goals, which means continual expansion to include new goals. And you need to achieve a congruence in your life that allows you to pursue both work and family goals.

We're now rounding the bend to the last chapter. This is where you'll learn what 1 percent performers have to teach you.

 Sales is an *expansion activity*. See how Coach Burt mental maps his weeks and *attacks* his days for maximum sales capacity.

CHAPTER 11

The Habit of 1 Percent Performers

How to Reignite Your Prey Drive and Be a Pro Every Single Day

Hide not your talents, they for use were made,
What's a sun-dial in the shade?

—BENJAMIN FRANKLIN

Somewhere along the way of coaching people, I began challenging them to go pro and leave their amateur desires behind. It became a rallying cry for me to challenge people to see the difference between the actions of an amateur and the actions of a professional and prompt them to want to make that transition. After all, we want to be the best at what we do, right? This requires not only a deep study of what makes the best the best, but also a commitment to do the deep work to make the jump from where we are to where we aspire to be. This will require sacrifice of something that could be valuable to you, whether that's time, energy, or money. Only you can decide how badly you want to be the best, understanding the benefits—and burdens—that come along with that decision.

So let's get started by studying the habits of the top 1 percent of performers in the world (a concept brought to me by my friend and famous sports psychologist Dr. Kevin Elko). This practice shows you the habits you need to acquire to play at the highest levels. Even having a desire to be in the top 1 percent requires an insatiable Prey Drive to begin with and an even bigger Prey Drive to stay the course. For many, overcoming their inertia to start is hard, and once started, the consistency to keep going also eludes many with one small sidetrack knocking people out of the game.

The following habits will give you a framework to make that desire to be in the top 1 percent a reality. And to be clear, this doesn't have to mean the 1 percent of money earners, but the top 1 percent of whatever you choose—firefighter, basketball coach, salesperson, or stay-at-home parent.

So let's take a look at the top habits of the 1 percent of performers (as listed in the Forbes 250 Study by *Forbes Magazine*). As we work through these, begin asking yourself which habits you lack and need to go to work on. And remember, all of this begins with a deep desire to be the best. Without tapping into this instinct, you may never really dig into these habits.

1. **REMARKABLE BOLDNESS.** I define boldness as striking and noticeable action without fear. When we talk about remarkable boldness, this could mean boldness in action, boldness in perspective, boldness in risk, or boldness in messaging. Those who make this a habit have clear beliefs and concepts about themselves that were developed along the way and are now hard (if

not impossible) to break. They take a stand and take action on what they believe in, many times with a polarizing outcome of people either loving them or hating them. They make big bets on themselves and are decisive—they are action takers. When these people see something that can help them, whether it's a book, a person, a strategy, or an adversary, they quickly take action. They know there are only two roads to go down: fail or fail forward. These people go all the way up the mountain and attract large numbers of people to them in the process (and typically repel large numbers of people at the same time).

2. **INTRINSIC MOTIVATION.** One-percenters have intrinsic motivation because their goals help them achieve something that matters. We've talked about Because Goals earlier in the book—these are the deeply intrinsic reasons that people take action even when they may not feel like it. Many times this deep motivation goes back to key revelations in people's lives where they observed something and as a result developed a concept, and "because of that" they take action. In essence, they "translate their mission to their moment." Remember, the Prey Drive is in us, but many times it is activated by something outside us that lights the fire. The top 1 percent have deeply entrenched reasons and concepts that are hard to be broken. An example would be something I say to myself: "Because when I was six years old, a coach believed in me, poured into me, and told me that one day I would be a great coach, I have devoted my entire life to helping other people." It's deep and intrinsic. It's not a feeling;

it's a motivation that runs deeper into the minds and hearts of people. When push comes to shove, these Because Goals allow people to fight through their feelings and emotions and take action.

3. **HIGH LEVELS OF RESILIENCE AND GRIT.** The top 1 percent just keep coming. Even in the toughest of situations, they rebound, thanks to resilience. Resilience is a mindset of "bounce back and grit." Every study in the world tells us that IQ, although valuable, is not the number one ingredient for success, but rather grit is. Our grit is a mix of passion (irresistible belief) and persistence (the second phase of the Prey Drive). Combined, resilience and grit are what help the 1 percent be able to take a hit and keep on ticking. It's the mindset of using adversity to actually accelerate progress versus remain stagnant. The top 1 percent cannot be broken. They always find a way to win. They expect things to be harder than they look and take longer than it would seem. This mindset is in place when they have to confront resistance or tension.

4. **CONNECTION AND FAMILY.** One-percenters treat everyone they interact with and come across the same way: they treat them like family. That type of connection is an art and a science. What it requires is lowering walls of resistance, being open and inviting, connecting to the heart and soul of another, and intrinsically validating people, and the 1 percent have perfected all of that. The top 1 percent are incredible with people. They have a heart to serve. They connect on an energy level, meaning you can sense and feel physically that they have your interest at heart and

are there to serve you. The top 1 percent work hard at developing the compassion and empathy for others that people can feel and connect with through the authenticity of the top 1 percent.

5. **ABILITY TO LOCK IN AND SEE IT THROUGH.** The top 1 percent have the ability to lock in and see something through to its conclusion. This means they have the staying power to stick with something until it is done. They focus on outcomes—on driving those outcomes and doing the nitty-gritty it takes to achieve the outcomes. Resistance doesn't faze them, nor does negativity. They turn resistance and negativity into a positive to find a better way. They cannot be easily distracted or "pulled apart" from their outcomes and have an uncanny ability to stay in there until complete.

These five habits tie directly into the activation and reactivation of your Prey Drive, as they illustrate how high achievers think and respond and what separates them from others. The ability to activate boldness inside you when you are afraid or to lock in and see something through to its conclusion is what distinguishes the very top performers in the world.

It is the intrinsic motivation that I believe comes from big Because Goals and the level of connection the top 1 percent have that serve to separate these people from the rest. When I'm evaluating what is keeping people from going from A to B in their lives, it typically comes down to one of these five things:

1. **KNOWLEDGE.** They don't know "how" to get there.
2. **SKILL.** Their skill is not refined enough.
3. **DESIRE.** This is the Prey Drive. They don't have enough of it.

4. **CONFIDENCE.** They don't believe they can do it.
5. **RELATIONSHIP.** They are not connected to "who" can help them, so they stay where they are.

What is it that they are lacking?

- Many are lacking boldness to take risk and action.
- Many are lacking a true connection to others that is substantial.
- Many are lacking the intrinsic motivation and resilience to start and finish.
- Many are lacking the grit it takes to do the nitty-gritty.

These habits and frameworks allow me as a coach to dig in and locate what could be prohibiting people from advancing confidently in the direction of their dreams.

———

Now that you understand the habits of the best of the best, let's take a look at some strategies that can help you keep your fire lit for long cycles of time so you can stay at the top.

The first step is to change the way you see yourself. The greats have cultivated an image of themselves that cannot be broken. They may get knocked down. They may get kicked while down. They may run into major opposition and resistance, but their image of who they are cannot be broken by any experiences.

I've worked with people who had a low-self-esteem and "I'm a failure" identity, and when push came to shove, they always found a way to contract to a place of comfort and could not perform under pressure. I've also worked with people who developed a confident and "get it done" identity, and you couldn't keep them down. They came with "batteries included" and always showed up ready to perform with no excuses.

What identity do you bring with you every day? Do you believe you are the best at what you do, or do you still perform like an amateur or somehow have impostor syndrome? Remember, the greats develop a positive identity of themselves, and that identity can't be broken by the failures they experience or other people's opinions of them.

I want you to see yourself like a top performer, salesperson, athlete, artist, or entertainer. I want you to see yourself like you are the best at what you do. I want you to know deep in your bones that your entire life is built around your unique skills and talents to maximize and enrich your life. You wake up and you perform, and when you perform, you do so at your highest level possible. The conditions are right (because you set them up that way), and you are primed and ready, and you dazzle people when you show up with your energy and your impression of increase.

You then rest and you rejuvenate. This is the state in which ideas are born. The inspiration comes. The vision is available to you when the mind is relaxed. You practice. You work your craft. You hone your talents. You work backstage to master your message.

All of that being said, there will be many days when you have to perform, but you just won't feel like it. That's OK, but the greats keep showing up. This is where you see that grit and resilience.

It takes both art and science to reignite your Prey Drive once you've lost it. It has a lot to do with a rhythm of life you create and live. Let's dive in and see how you create a pulse to the way you live, giving you greater and greater levels of enjoyment in life versus stress and anxiety.

TAKING THE PULSE OF YOUR PREY DRIVE

Oxford Languages defines the word "rejuvenation" as "the action or process of giving new energy or vigor to something," and this is incredibly fitting, as your Prey Drive will need to be rejuvenated by continual reactivation. This will take specific actions on your part. What actions?

First, each morning you must get up with the determination to fight another day. You must initiate, start, and rev the engine.

Second, you have to spend time recharging, and for me the best time to do this is on the weekends. How you spend your weekends has a great deal to do with how you launch into the week. It took me a while to mature to this, but once I did, it changed everything for me.

For example, between ages 20 and 30, I pushed hard and played harder. I coached, drank way too much alcohol, and chased too many good times. I spent entire weekends hung over or messing around. The hard work through the week with intense stress and pressure prompted me on the weekends to always look for outlets of fun that were unhealthy. Although I was a good coach, I was distracted by so many things. I was not a pro.

Finally, in my mid-thirties, I decided to leave behind my amateur desires and to go pro, with a focus on my body, mind, heart, and spirit. When you decide to make this change, your weekends become a time for you to restore all four parts of your nature. On weekends, I study how successful people relax, I spend valuable time with my family, and generally I don't have a schedule to follow. I personally like studying documentaries, taking bike rides where I listen to podcasts, and experiencing general periods of what I call "creative loafing," which is just allowing my mind to go wherever it wants to roam with no schedule.

Strategies like these reactivate your drive and allow you to be significantly better when you come in on Monday than you were the week before. Average folks come in on Monday exactly the way they left on Friday and typically can't figure out why they can't get any new results. One-percenters start Monday substantially better than when they left because of how they used their weekend and time off to allow this creative process to manifest.

To sum up, how you spend your weekend matters. The constant process of activating and reactivating your drive is invaluable to the pro. You need the rest. You need the creativity. You need the time to decompress and regenerate, or else you just replicate.

I suggest trying these strategies in a coming weekend:

- **FRIDAY NIGHT.** Rest and spend time with your family or by yourself. Totally decompress. Shut work off.
- **SATURDAY (OR YOUR DAY OFF).** Do whatever you want to do. Study someone great by reading interviews, books, and articles and/or by watching documentaries about the person. I watch a documentary (for fun), study someone who did something big, or read for inspiration. When you do this, it will expand your mind and open up the dreamer in you. You can be creative because you are not in the rat race. The dreamer in you needs to be reactivated and needs the important time off.
- **SUNDAY (AFTER YOUR SPIRITUAL TIME).** Draw or mentally map your week. Design your big moves. Get creative. Let your mind play. Think *big*. Don't worry

about the mechanics of your dreams. Just draw and redraw; paint pictures in your mind. Spend a lot of time asking yourself who can help you move from A to B.

On top of this weekend "schedule," I also sit down each night of the week and map out my next day using a system I created called the Monster Growth System (first described in my book *Legacy Selling*); it consists of a set of actions a person can take to drive up the probability of making a sale and creating new income. This process and growth system activates and reactivates my drive because it takes me to a place in the future that both fascinates me and excites me, and it refocuses my time and energy on my biggest opportunities. It helps me take all the ideas of relationships and concepts and place them in a mental construct to play offense rather than defense. It keeps me in creation mode because it keeps me focused on the future and not on the past.

I start by drawing up these concepts for structure:

- What is the biggest *Level 10* opportunity available to me? This is the biggest opportunity available to me that I need to be focused on.
- I then move to my *Blue Marlin* relationships, my biggest relationships. These are relationships with people who are typically key influencers who have access to large numbers of new people. How can I help them, or how can they help me move toward our dominant aspiration?
- I then move to my *Red Zone* of people who are close to making a buying decision. These are people who are just "at rest" and need to be contacted and converted to a deal.

- I then move to my *Farm Club*, which represents people who have indicated interest but have yet to take an action and need to be "cultivated."
- I then move to my *Hit List*, which represents people I believe my team and I can help with our services. These people could be strategic partners, current clients, current leads, or potential leads.
- I then move to my *Top 25*, which represent 25 powerful relationships with people who can introduce my team and I to new people (these are powerful feeder systems of opportunity). Remember, the key to the many is to the one. The strategy here is to feed into these relationships to open new doors of opportunity.
- I then move to my *Net Promoters* or new clients that need to be onboarded correctly to make it a good experience, so we can help them move from A to B in their lives.
- I then move to my *Showcase* events, which are events I'm planning so I can bring people together to activate and reactivate our relationships. You will never go wrong by bringing people together.

You may be wondering how I execute all of the preceding. I take this system, and I focus on it for a minimum of two hours per day to create our daily numbers. It would be broken down daily to these numbers:

- 1–3 Level 10 opportunities
- 3–5 Blue Marlins
- 5 Red Zones
- 5 Farm Clubs
- 5 Hit Lists

- 3–10 Net Promoters
- 1–3 Showcase events being planned at all times

This would equal roughly 36 high-value activities per day. These high-value activities are activities I would take to drive up the probability of success. Compare those with just a few activities or with low-value activities, and you can see that you will be way ahead of everyone else. This gets me playing offense. This gets my Prey Drive activated.

Remember our motto: When in doubt, take an action. This system gives you lots of actions to take.

———

Now let's focus on moving you from a reactive standpoint of wasting and escaping on the weekends to playing offense and using the weekends to recommit and rejuvenate. We spend one weekend day mapping out the system, and each night to program the subconscious mind we sit down and rework the system again and again. When we get to work on Monday, we execute on the system.

Each weekend is a time to:

- Get intentional.
- Make a decision to come to work every day refreshed and ready to perform.
- Set targets and get serious about them.
- Program your subconscious mind to perform. Tell your brain that this is what is going to happen.
- Really go pro versus stay in an amateur position and keep getting amateur results.

Begin to treat yourself like an athlete. *You rest. You practice. You perform.* And you perform at the highest possible levels, which requires rest.

Remember, the first sale you have got to make every day is the one to yourself.

Tell yourself this: "I am a person of interest. People are counting on me to show up, to grow up, and to deliver. My positive energy will be greater than any negative energy I may face today." And remember, athletes get tired, entertainers burn out, and coaches move on to new jobs. You have to get above the noise and your feelings and learn how to show up even when you are tired, even when you are exhausted, even when you don't feel like it. We don't feel our way into acting; we act our way into feeling.

Another way to ensure you rejuvenate yourself enough is ensuring you fight past resistance. When you reach for big goals and big dreams, you will meet resistance. Resistance in thought, resistance from others, or just resistance because you are in a place you've never been before. This can cause you to retreat because it's uncomfortable. Utilizing this resistance to instead accelerate progress is key to reactivating the drive inside you. This is a skill you can develop, but it takes work and awareness. If you are knocked down, let it be only for a day; then reactivate that drive. Learn to use adversity as a competitor, or as an activator to reactivate. I do this, and I teach my clients to do this by initiating self-talk that looks like this:

- "I'm only looking for people who are looking for me."
- "I am going to go where I feel celebrated, not tolerated."
- "I don't have to live with rejection. Some will; some won't; so what."

- "There is no shortage of money or opportunity; yet there is a shortage of confidence and conviction."
- "I don't need more money; I need more people, and there are over 7 billion people in the world."
- "I will stay in creation versus catastrophe mode."

The point here is that there is no loss, only gain. You gain your resistance, challenges, and setbacks. Everything is a gain when you train your mind to think that way.

———

Different people need different things; different people find rejuvenation in different places. The point is that your drive has to be reactivated every day. For you, it may be exposure to bigger things that you get from listening to or watching something that motivates you. It may be changing your state through physical exercise or a changing your environment. It may be a routine you need to get back into. Whatever that is for you, you need to discover the best way to rejuvenate and work to get in a peak flow state as often as possible. Being under high degrees of stress or burnout deactivates the drive and takes us out of creation and into catastrophe.

DON'T BE A ONE-HIT WONDER

Now that you have gotten this far, I hope that you're remembering these principles and the tools, concepts, and resources you've learned about and that you are using them every single day. Never underestimate the need to activate and reactivate your drive every single day. The one thing vital to longevity is to be able to "play ball" each and every time at the highest levels. The greats have this. You have to cultivate it if you want to be incredible.

When you can't or don't reactivate your drive, you are in danger of becoming the "one-hit wonder" that climbs the mountain one time—you've run out of resolve and no longer have the drive to ever climb another mountain. This is what separates the true professionals from the amateurs. The pros keep finding a way to win—they keep writing hits and winning games. The amateurs win one time and think, "I did enough."

Remember, big-time people use their weekends to reactivate their Prey Drive. Small-time people use their weekends to escape from the week. *And remember*, you are not average. You are a warrior. You have the Prey Drive of a *champion*. I believe in you . . .

WHAT WE LEARNED AND WHAT'S NEXT

To know how to reactivate your drive and rejuvenate your life is to know how to bring something that is dormant back to life. It is the ability to spark an interest in something. It really is the ability to flip the switch and move into performance mode. Planning and action typically do this.

When you show up, you need to do it in a way that deeply impacts other people. You need to show up in such a way that others will never forget you. To show up and really transform the lives of other people, you have to be playing at a very high level yourself.

You, as a top 1 percent person, should be interested in self-actualization, reaching your deepest human potential:

This starts with you being interested in you.

This starts with how you spend your time.

This starts with you making a simple decision to go pro.

This starts with you and how you work and flow and recommit.

This starts with you activating and reactivating your drive every single day.

Now let's leave our amateur desires behind and be a one-percenter in every part of our lives. *Flip the switch!*

 Watch Coach Burt's *live* presentation to 3,000 people on "Habits of the Top 1% of Performers."

Afterword

At 45 years old, I've tried to understand what much of the purpose of my life has been. As a young coach in athletics, I was always motivated and fascinated by activating an energy inside people to help them believe in themselves so they could activate their own potential. Many times I see something in them before they see it in themselves.

I consistently say to audiences around the world that we don't find our why or purpose; it finds us. It finds us when we are "in the game" or in the arena doing and pursuing. It finds us when we are "working the muscle" and pushing toward something that interests us. We are using our talents to solve a problem, and this creates an exchange of energy and a feedback loop that is positive and fulfilling. It activates and reactivates.

At 41 I believe my purpose discovered me, and it was what I had been doing my entire life—and that is activating the Prey Drive in another person. In my opinion nothing happens in life until this one thing is activated. This is what I've been doing for over 30 years now, activating a deep drive within people that opens them up to their own possibility, their own talents, their own potential, and their own bigger future.

A person on my team said to me one day, "When people are with you, they are awakened to their own bigger possibilities, and you help them believe they can achieve them." This is the activation of your Prey Drive. First you see it, and then you pursue it with a persistence and intensity all the way through to its conclusion. A good coach is a professional reminder of what we need to do every single day.

I firmly believe that until the Prey Drive is activated, nothing happens, because there is no hunger for expansion. There is no hunger for growth. There is no hunger for improvement. Satisfaction in life breeds a comfort in us and starves out the drive that we so desperately need to break through.

You have to find that drive again if you plan on realizing your potential. You have to locate the activator of your drive or you remain static versus dynamic. Remember, *the pursuit is the reward*. It's not the trophy, the money, the status, or the fame. In the animal there is no greater motivator than the instinct to satiate a hunger. This is you pursuing your potential in all four parts of your nature—the body, the mind, the heart, and the spirit.

I believe God has given us talent and potential as a gift. It is up to us to activate that potential and step into that potential and do something with that potential. In the Garden of Eden, God said to Adam, "Work the garden and take care of it." From the beginning we were to tend to, work, and create. All of this takes a drive. All of this takes an action. All of this takes movement.

My hope is this book goes deep into your soul and helps you find a talent and potential that has been latent and undeveloped and put it to good use. I hope it helps you initiate a movement toward a bigger future. Please send me your success stories along the way and know that I believe in you . . . I believe in the potential and power of people. And I believe that potential has no age or boundaries. It's just there waiting for you to utilize it. It is now time for you to put your drive into action to achieve the freakish level of success you were destined to create.

Everybody needs a coach in life . . . thank you for letting me be yours,

Coach Micheal Burt
Nashville, Tennessee

 Activate your Prey Drive with Coach Burt coaching you and your team, or come to a live event.

Notes

Chapter 1

1. Stephen R. Covey, *The 8th Habit: From Effectiveness to Greatness*, Free Press, New York, 2004.
2. Stephen R. Covey, *The 7 Habits of Highly Effective People*, Simon & Schuster, New York, 1989.

Chapter 2

1. Steven Kotler, *The Art of Impossible: A Peak Performance Primer*, Harper Wave, New York, 2021.
2. While working on my doctorate, I had a course in quantitative and qualitative measurement. I couldn't understand why a leadership degree required this until I began my coaching businesses. A quantitative goal is one you can measure. It's tangible. A qualitative goal is one you can feel yet can't measure. I believe you need both to help you with your B. For example, I have Bs that are measurable and Bs that I can feel (for instance, I'm happier with less stress or doing what I love).

Chapter 3

1. Steven Kotler, *The Art of Impossible: A Peak Performance Primer*, Harper Wave, New York, 2021.

Chapter 4

1. Steven Kotler, *The Art of Impossible: A Peak Performance Primer*, Harper Wave, New York, 2021.

Chapter 5

1. James Champy and Nitin Nohria, *The Arc of Ambition: Defining the Leadership Journey*, Basic Books, New York, 2000.

Chapter 7

1. Cal Newport, *Deep Work: Rules for Focused Success in a Distracted World*, Grand Central Publishing, New York, 2016.

Chapter 9

1. Steven Kotler, *The Art of Impossible: A Peak Performance Primer*, Harper Wave, New York, 2021.

Chapter 10

1. Tim S. Grover, *Winning: The Unforgiving Race to Greatness*, Scribner, New York, 2021.

Index

About the Author

COACH MICHEAL BURT is considered the leading authority on activating the *Prey Drive* in people and teams around the world. Coach Burt defines "Prey Drive" in this context as "an instinctual ability to see something either with the eyes or in the mind and have the persistence and intensity to pursue it."

Based on his unique background as a former championship women's basketball coach combined with his impressive ability to build a "competitive intelligence" in people, this author of 17 books uses a unique methodology to inner-engineer people to compete at the highest levels. Coach Burt goes to work on all four parts of a person's nature through building specific knowledge for the mind, impeccable skills for the body, intense desire for the heart, and a contagious confidence for the spirit.

Hired by many of the top companies and top-performance individuals in the world to activate this drive, Coach Burt has built out a framework and model to *flip the switch* in people, resulting in quantitative improvements in concentrated periods of time. Currently Coach Burt is building and licensing Greatness Factories around the world, which are unique destination locations that combine "intentional collaboration" between members through inspired real estate, coaching programs, and a common desire to do something *legendary*.